The Legacy of
Fort William Henry

THE LEGACY OF
Fort William Henry

RESURRECTING THE PAST

David R. Starbuck

UNIVERSITY PRESS OF NEW ENGLAND ✳ HANOVER AND LONDON

University Press of New England

www.upne.com

© 2014 University Press of New England

All rights reserved

Manufactured in the United States of America

Designed by April Leidig

Typeset in Minion by Copperline Book Services, Inc.

For permission to reproduce any of the material in this book, contact Permissions, University Press of New England, One Court Street, Suite 250, Lebanon NH 03766; or visit www.upne.com

Library of Congress Cataloging-in-Publication Data

Starbuck, David R.

The legacy of Fort William Henry: resurrecting the past / David R. Starbuck.

pages cm

Includes index.

ISBN 978-1-61168-547-3 (pbk.: alk. paper)

ISBN 978-1-61168-548-0 (ebook)

1. Fort William Henry (N.Y.) — Antiquities. 2. Excavations (Archaeology) — New York (State) — Fort William Henry. 3. New York (State) — History — French and Indian War, 1754–1763 — Antiquities. 4. United States — History — French and Indian War, 1754–1763 — Antiquities. 5. Fort William Henry (N.Y.) — Capture, 1757. I. Title.

E199.S785 2014

974.7'51 — dc23   2013043809

5 4 3 2 1

Frontis, page iii: Face of Burial 14.
Courtesy of Anthony Reynolds.

CONTENTS

PREFACE

What makes a fort "great"? What causes it to be remembered for hundreds of years? How can the events that occurred at a frontier fort change the course of a war and make it one of the signature events in American history? And how do we avoid all of the myths and fanciful stories that surround a famous historical event?

More than ten years ago I published *Massacre at Fort William Henry* (Starbuck 2002), an overview of the history and archeology of America's early frontier fort at the southern end of Lake George, New York. So much has been learned since then that it is now time to tell a "newer" story of the fort, reporting on the archeological and forensic findings that are gradually changing our perceptions of events at this fascinating point of conflict between the British and French empires in America. The fort's history has certainly not changed — no new caches of historical documents have been found — but the physical remains discovered at the ruins of Fort William Henry are most definitely changing the ways in which we view life at the fort prior to the massacre of 1757. This is very much an archeological story, to be told by those who have sifted through the remains of the fort and who have come to admire the men who served here so long ago.

This is also a local story for me because I grew up about twenty miles north of the modern village of Lake George. As a child I often visited the recreated fort, viewed the exhibits, enjoyed the guided tours, and purchased toy cannons in the gift shop. I was too young in 1953 and 1954 to be able to remember now whether I ever actually visited the archeological excavations at that time, but I am sure I never anticipated that one day I would be privileged to direct my own excavations both inside and outside the fort. I began digging through the ruins of Fort William Henry some sixteen years ago, and I would argue that I now have a nearly unique perspective on the soldiers and officers who served here, a personal bond with the fort's defenders that is rich and deep. Digging in the dirt where soldiers fought and died has made Fort William Henry come alive for me as a three-dimensional adventure filled with mystery, sadness, and death.

I would like to thank the Fort William Henry Corporation, the State University of New York Adirondack, and Plymouth State University for sponsoring our field and laboratory work at Fort William Henry between 1997 and 2000, and again in 2011 and 2012. I am grateful to the Fort William Corporation for permission to use many of the images that are in their collections. Thanks are also due to well over 100 students, volunteers, and staff members who joined in the research. Although it is not possible to mention everyone who participated in our field crews over the years, these individuals have been an amazing group to work with, and they all deserve praise for helping to tell the story of this history-making fort. There is always something new to be learned by digging in the ground!

I would especially like to thank the management and staff of the Fort William Henry Corporation for their many kindnesses throughout our work: Robert Flacke Sr., Kathy Muncil, Melodie Viele, Tom Cushing, Anne Hunter, Shawn Tuller, Mike Sabo, Suzanne Mills, Gerald Bradfield, Pam and Steve Collyer, Bruce Nelson, Robert Frasier, Rebecca Barrett, Mechylle Hammond, the late Dawn Littrell, Dan Donahue, and all of the other guides and interpreters at the fort. I would also like to thank Sarah Majot, who directed digs there in 2005; Carleton Dunn, who was first hired by the fort in 1953 and who continues to be a frequent source of invaluable information; and the board members of the French and Indian War Society: Fred Austin, Joseph Zarzynski, the late John Farrell, Jack Kokoletsos, John Strough, and Dale Erhardt. Our field supervisors on the summer digs have included the late John Farrell, Matthew Rozell, Brad Jarvis, Andy Farry, Gordon and Barbara DeAngelo, Lauren Sheridan, John Strough, John Kosek, Susan Winchell-Sweeney, Sarah van Ryckevorsel, Claudia Young, Judy Balyeat, Nia Alecksynas, and Justin Sturges. Their dedication and supervisory skills have been essential throughout our work.

In addition, I would like to thank those who worked in our summer field laboratories, especially Elizabeth "Betty" Hall, Merle Parsons, Maureen Kennedy, and June Talley. Together they oversaw the processing of many thousands of artifacts. Betty Hall has spent hundreds, perhaps thousands, of hours over many winters identifying the artifacts we uncovered and entering the information into a database on a computer, often assisted by Work Study students from Plymouth State University.

Dr. Victoria Bunker of Alton, New Hampshire, examined hundreds of prehistoric pottery sherds found at the fort, and her comments were most helpful. Timothy Todish of Grand Rapids, Michigan, and George Bray of Rochester, New York, have been a wonderful source of historical information for all things pertaining to the French and Indian War. And James Richardson III of the Carnegie Museum of Natural History provided some fascinating insights into his own excavations at the fort in the 1950s.

I am grateful to Karen T. Taylor, a forensic specialist who operates her business, Facial Images, in Austin, Texas. It was she who assessed the skull of Burial 14 and developed frontal and lateral drawings based on her morphological observations and experience in forensic identification cases. Taylor incorporated the anthropological findings of Dr. Kate Spradley and Dr. Michelle Hamilton from the Forensic Anthropology Center at Texas State University. Based on Taylor's reconstruction drawings, Tony Reynolds then converted her images to 3D digital form. Their reconstructions of the face of Burial 14 are a very significant contribution to this book.

I owe special thanks to Jene Romeo for contributing appendix 2 to this book. Jene has studied the animal bones recovered from the fort over several years, and her work will form the basis of her doctoral dissertation.

Finally, I would like to thank the thousands of visitors to our excavations who have shared their ideas, their interpretations, and their enthusiasm for our archeological findings. Having an appreciative audience always makes the work go better. When *Massacre at Fort William Henry* was published in 2002, I was approached in the parking lot at the fort by a total stranger, who asked me, "Is your book politically correct? I won't buy it if it is." I assured him that it was not, wondering, of course, whether he feared that I might be one of those who have made too many "revisions" to traditional American history. But this is a warning to every author. We must tell the story of politically charged events as honestly as possible, in this case presenting French, Native American, and British actions in an evenhanded way. The historiography of Fort William Henry is most fascinating, with every generation telling the story in new ways that reflect the political, racial, and moral attitudes of the moment. There is no hidden truth waiting to be discovered at this fort. Rather, there are many points of view, and I believe that my role is to add an archeological perspective to the dialogue, teasing insights from the soil where soldiers fought and died so many years ago.

David R. Starbuck
JULY 2013

The Legacy of
Fort William Henry

The Brief Life of a Frontier Fort

THIS IS HOW Fort William Henry first appeared to Hawk-eye, the noble protagonist in James Fenimore Cooper's 1826 novel, *The Last of the Mohicans*. Then, the edge of Lake George lay somewhat closer to the fort than it does today, and the "entrenched camp" located to the southeast contained reinforcements recently arrived from Fort Edward, sent by Major General Daniel Webb to bolster the British position at the southern end of Lake George. (These were Massachusetts troops and the 60th [Royal American] Regiment of Foot, and they camped within what is now the Lake George Battlefield Park.)

Cooper and his contemporaries recognized that in August of 1757 this strategically positioned frontier fort had become the setting for the most horrific events of the French and Indian War, when a small British garrison was assaulted by a vastly superior force of French and Indians. Cooper was one of early America's greatest authors, and *The Last of the Mohicans* helped define for his time what it meant to be an American.

Introduction

Because *The Legacy of Fort William Henry* is largely about new findings, I do not wish to retell stories that may already be all too familiar. There currently are several excellent book-length treatments of the history of Fort William Henry, including *Betrayals* (Steele 1990), *The Siege of Fort William Henry* (Hughes 2011), *Massacre at Fort William Henry* (Starbuck 2002), and *Relief Is Greatly Wanted* (Dodge 1998). Shorter, chapter-length descriptions of the fort appear in *Empires in the Mountains* (Bellico 2010), *Chronicles of Lake George: Journeys in War and Peace* (Bellico 1995), *The Great Warpath* (Starbuck 1999b), and *The Archaeology of Forts and Battlefields* (Starbuck 2011); and pertinent articles have been published by Timothy Todish (1993), Brenda Baker and Christina Rieth (2000), Maria Liston and Brenda Baker (1995), and myself (1990, 1993, 1998, 2001, and 2008).

Fort William Henry, the northernmost British outpost in the colony of New York during the 1750s, has major significance in American history as the first bastioned British fort in the North American colonies, with French-style bastions in all four corners that helped catch enemy attackers

1.1. (*Above*)
A drawing of the proposed reconstruction of Fort William Henry. Fort William Henry Museum.

1.2. (*Right*)
An old print of "Lake George" by P. Hinshelwood. New York: D. Appleton.

in a crossfire (fig. 1.1). The log fort faced north, toward a French enemy that had also laid claim to Lake George (fig. 1.2), and thus military conflict was almost inevitable. Fort William Henry came under siege on August 3, 1757, by French and Indians newly arrived from Fort Carillon (later renamed Fort Ticonderoga). Constructed just two years earlier, Fort William Henry was subjected to a steadily worsening bombardment for six days as siege

1.3. The southwest bastion of Fort William Henry as the reconstructed fort appears today (2012). Note the small white "cloud" on the left, which is smoke rising from a newly fired cannon.

trenches and cannon fire grew ever closer. The fort's garrison suffered heavy casualties, even as its commander, Irish-born Lieutenant Colonel George Monro, waited nearby in the entrenched camp of reinforcements. The fort's subsequent surrender and the massacre that followed were later described in *The Last of the Mohicans*, and in that sad distinction, the fall of Fort William Henry became the single best-remembered event of the French and Indian War. The French army then destroyed the fort with fire before they returned to Fort Carillon. Since gruesome events are far more likely to be remembered than architectural innovations or stories about daily life on the American frontier, the destruction of Fort William Henry will no doubt be memorialized for centuries to come.

Fortunately, archeology conducted in the 1950s enabled this bastioned timber fort to rise again as a popular international attraction (fig. 1.3). In the twenty-first century, Fort William Henry continues to greet modern visitors from its beautiful, high terrace overlooking Lake George, called the "Queen of American Lakes." This reconstructed fort provides fascinating information about eighteenth-century military life, even as it tells one of the grimmest stories of warfare on the American frontier.

Historical Context

In 1646 Father Isaac Jogues named this body of water Lac du St. Sacrement and claimed it for France, marking the first European intrusion into the region (fig. 1.4). In later years, French and British armies turned much of

1.4. Exhibit dedicated to Father Isaac Jogues on the second floor of the North Barracks, now relocated to the first floor.

what is now northern New York State into a vast battlefield as they fought for control of North America and, indeed, much of the world. The French and Indian War was one of many American wars in the eighteenth century, and less famous struggles such as King William's War, Queen Anne's War, and King George's War provided a foretaste of the fight of George Washington and the Virginia militia against the French in July 1754 at Fort Necessity in Pennsylvania, followed by the Battle of Lake George in the following year.

The Battle of Lake George on September 8, 1755, brought war to the northernmost parts of the colony of New York and pitted the British under General William Johnson against the French under Jean Erdman, Baron Dieskau. In bloody fighting, both Colonel Ephraim Williams and King Hendrick, the Mohawk leader, were killed, but the British held the field of battle at the end of the day. What followed was a fort-building race, as the French began construction of Fort Carillon thirty-five miles north on Lake Champlain, and Captain William Eyre of the 44th Regiment of Foot — following the orders of General Johnson — began construction of Fort William Henry at the southern end of Lake George. A far larger British base, Fort Edward, was simultaneously constructed about sixteen miles to the south, and the two British forts faced off against the French for the next two years.

Eyre became the first commander of Fort William Henry, and he designed the fort with four log barracks buildings (with casemate rooms underneath), storehouses, officers' quarters, a hospital, a powder magazine, and sheds, all of which lay within a central parade ground. A dry moat flanked the fort on three sides, and thirty-foot-thick walls of earth and logs surrounded the whole. Diamond-shaped bastions were constructed at the corners, and entry into the fort was via a bridge that crossed the moat. A "necessary" for human waste was located at the northeast corner of the fort. The location of the log fort put it in danger from the outset: it was on land claimed by the French. The garrison of between 2,200 and 2,300 was a mixture of British and provincial soldiers and included a company of the 35th Regiment, a company of the 42nd Highlanders, two companies of the 44th Regiment of Foot, and two companies of the 48th Regiment of Foot. Ranger units were also present, including Speakman's Company, Hobb's Company, and Richard Rogers's Company. Their leader, Lieutenant Colonel George Monro of the 35th Regiment, was a career soldier and a Scotsman.

During the two-year face-off between the French and British forts, there was just one serious attack on Fort William Henry. About 1,600 French and Indians, led by Canadian Governor-General François-Pierre de Rigaud de Vaudreuil, attacked the fort on March 19, 1757, and then destroyed the New Jersey Regiment (called the Jersey Blues) at Sabbath Day Point on Lake George. Finally, in August 1757, General Louis-Joseph de Montcalm-Gozon, Marquis de Saint-Veran, led an army against the fort that included between eight and ten thousand French regulars, Canadian militia, and Indians. Most traveled down the lake in bateaux and artillery rafts; others traveled by land down the west side of Lake George.

General Montcalm sent a letter to Colonel Monro, requesting that he surrender, and when Monro refused, the French proceeded to construct entrenchments that partially encircled the fort. The siege began on August 3. British cannons and mortars gave out, ammunition ran low, and the British surrender finally came on August 9. Given the brave British defense, the French granted generous terms of capitulation appropriate to European-style warfare, and the British garrison promised not to take up arms against the French for the next eighteen months. They were allowed to take their (unloaded) weapons with them, and in the aftermath of the surrender, the British garrison was escorted through the eastern gate of the fort under a French armed guard that probably consisted of about three hundred soldiers. The British army spent that night in the entrenched camp southeast of the fort and departed for Fort Edward early on the following day, August 10.

It was then that some of Montcalm's Indian allies (Abenakis from Canada) killed and scalped the sick and injured, after which they attacked the retreating soldiers on the Military Road that ran to Fort Edward. The French escort utterly failed to protect their British prisoners, more of whom were killed and scalped. Some escaped into the woods and eventually made their way to Fort Edward, and hundreds of others were subsequently dragged away as prisoners to Canada, where they were held for ransom. Ian Steele

(1990) has argued that the massacre switched fairly quickly from the killing of victims to the taking of prisoners.

Early chroniclers claimed that as many as 1,500 British were killed, but more recent analyses — based on period documents — have numbered the dead at the time of the massacre between 185 (Steele 1990, 143) and 308 (Dodge 1998, 97). A series of misunderstandings and betrayals had led to the post-surrender murder of many of the fort's defenders, and modern historians point out that Montcalm's Indian allies — who came from as many as forty different tribes — had been promised scalps and plunder in exchange for their participation in the expedition from Canada. The surrender agreement worked out between Montcalm and Monro effectively prevented Indians from receiving any booty, and the attack on the prisoners, the so-called massacre, was a belated attempt to obtain trophies and honor.

After the surrender, the French removed any supplies they could use, burned the fort to the ground on August 11 and 12, and then returned to Fort Carillon. Most then went north to Canada for the winter. After the siege, some of the Indians who had accompanied Montcalm dug into the graves in the military cemetery that lay outside the fort's walls, scalped the corpses, and stole blankets and clothing. Among the dead who were disinterred and mutilated was Richard Rogers, one of the brothers of the famed Major Robert Rogers who had raised and commanded Rogers' Rangers (Rogers 2002). Richard Rogers was one of those in the cemetery who had died from highly contagious diseases, and smallpox contracted from the cemetery was transmitted to Indians, who carried it along the trails running north to Canada. The smallpox that those who made it home brought with them led to the death of thousands of Indians in eastern Canada, as the disease decimated entire villages. It may be argued that the violation of Richard Rogers's body was a powerful motivation for Robert Rogers's attack on the Abenaki village of Saint Francis (Odanak) two years later — no doubt Robert believed himself to be justified in avenging his brother.

The surrender of the British garrison to Montcalm provided the basis for James Fenimore Cooper's *The Last of the Mohicans*, and the popularity of Cooper's highly fictionalized account has lingered in modern movies and memorabilia. The protagonists — Hawk-eye (also known as Natty Bumppo), Uncas, Chingachgook, the Huron Magua, and Colonel Monro's two beautiful daughters (Cora and Alice) — are probably better known than many of the commanding officers of that period. Movies and television shows have perpetuated old stereotypes and created new ones, and the 1936 movie version of Cooper's novel, with Randolph Scott, and the 1992 version, with Daniel Day-Lewis, are but two of many interpretations of the story. None of these characters ever existed, of course, and there is no clear evidence as to whether Colonel Monro ever married or had daughters. Monro survived the siege but lived only three months longer, dying of apoplexy on an Albany street on November 3, 1757.

In June 1758, the army of General James Abercromby camped on what had been the entrenched camp southeast of the fort and built an earthwork (with cannons) on the ruins of Fort William Henry. This was prior to Abercromby's failed attack on Fort Carillon on July 8 of that year. In July 1759 General Jeffery Amherst's army burned the ruins of Fort William Henry and spread clean dirt on top before he successfully captured Fort Carillon and renamed it Ticonderoga. Much of the war came to a conclusion on September 13, 1759, with General James Wolfe's attack on Quebec, the capital of New France, and the subsequent surrender of that city to the British a few days later. Both Wolfe and Montcalm were killed in that engagement (Parkman 1962), and just a few weeks later, on October 6, Rogers's Rangers attacked the village of Saint Francis (Odanak) and essentially ended the recurring Indian attacks that had plagued British settlements for years (Rogers 2002; Zaboly 2004). There was little military action after that date, although Montreal fell to the British on September 8, 1760. Finally, in 1763, the Treaty of Paris formally ended the French and Indian War, and with it many of France's claims to the North American continent.

Interest in Fort William Henry was by no means over, however, for in August 1783 General George Washington visited the site while on an inspection tour and walked over the ruins. In 1826 *The Last of the Mohicans* sparked renewed interest, but the ruins of the fort were increasingly neglected. A few paths ran across the surface of the fort, and much later a gazebo was added (fig. 1.5). The top of the fort's well continued to peek above the surface of the ground, which it has continued to do up until the present day. Fortunately, the dormancy of the site did not last, and the stage was being set for a renewal of interest in the fort and its tragic story (see chapter 3).

Lasting Consequences

The Marquis de Montcalm brought with him to Fort William Henry Indians from a great many nations in eastern Canada whose primary goal was to obtain scalps and plunder from the British. These included representatives of the Huron, Abenaki, Algonkin, Potawatomi, Ottawa, Iroquois, Nipissing, Ojibwa, Mississauga, Menominee, Winnebago, Sauk, Amalicite, Fox, Iowa, Loup, Puant, Delaware, and Micmac. Some had traveled as much as 1,500 miles while en route to Lake George. Many of these were peoples who had never fought together as allies before, and in hindsight it is amazing that Montcalm believed he could control such a disparate fighting force. Given the multitude of cultural and linguistic differences, this was a nearly impossible task, and one result was the massacre of British prisoners.

1.5. "SITE OF OLD
FORT WILLIAM HENRY
LAKE GEORGE."
A "PHOSTINT" CARD.
In this view of the
surface of the fort site
in 1910, a newly built
gazebo appears on the
right, the Fort William
Henry Hotel is in the
background, and the
top of the fort's well is
on the left.

The brutal events that destroyed Fort William Henry in the 1750s are highly charged for all sides even today, so it is easy to understand why the story of the massacre at Fort William Henry continues to fascinate, given its mix of racial and cultural tension and violence. But the facts of the story have become muddled in the minds of many because the fictional events and characters created by Cooper have outweighed the reality of what occurred at the fort. So it is that archeology, with its emphasis on physical survivals, may have the greatest ability to bring back to us some measure of reality. After all, would visitors to the fort rather hear a repetition of Cooper's story, or can archeology and public education offer something better: stories about the buildings, clothing, armaments, and food of ordinary soldiers and officers, coupled with physical evidence that shows us what actually survived after the final assault on the fort?

Beginnings

Native Americans on Lake George

WHEN FORT WILLIAM HENRY was being reconstructed in the 1950s, Native American hearths and prehistoric artifacts were found virtually everywhere on the fort grounds, and some of the best of these finds are on exhibit at the fort today in both the East and the North Barracks (fig. 2.1). Clearly Native Americans had been traveling and camping along the shores of Lake George for many thousands of years, and the story of their lives has the potential to be just as interesting as that of the soldiers who lived at the fort.

The early residents of the area were most likely the ancestors of the Mohicans (also known as Mahicans), who during the early historic period occupied the waterways that lie between New York State and Vermont, from the southern end of Lake Champlain south to what is now New York City and east into the Berkshires of Massachusetts (Dunn 1994). Their villages were surrounded by stockades and were usually located on hilltops for defense, but it was necessary for villages to be moved frequently as farmland and firewood became exhausted. The Mohicans typically relied on horticulture and fishing, with the women planting and tending the crops while the men fished, gathered mussels, and hunted.

Included in the 1950s collections housed at the fort are numerous examples of projectile points (spear points and arrowheads) from nearly all time periods in the past ten thousand years (fig. 2.2), demonstrating that Native Americans were living in the area by at least 8000–6000 B.C., and they were present almost continuously until Europeans arrived. Most notable among these finds are rare bifurcate-base projectile points (the type sometimes referred to as Kanawha) from the Early Archaic Period, and these are accompanied by ground stone tools (chiefly axes), caches of blades (fig. 2.3), a ground slate knife like an ulu, and a great many sherds of Native American pottery.

Our own more recent excavations (1997 to present), conducted under the auspices of the State University of New York Adirondack, have exposed further evidence of extensive Native American settlements both inside and outside the reconstructed fort, and clearly the British soldiers and officers who served here were not the first visitors to Lake George. Between 1997 and

2.1. (*Top*)
A recreated Iroquois longhouse on the first floor of the East Barracks.

2.2. (*Bottom*)
Stone tools excavated in the 1950s on display on the first floor of the East Barracks.

2000, we discovered prehistoric occupation layers nearly everywhere just beneath the surface of the parade ground, and then much deeper deposits outside the eastern wall of the fort. During our 2011–12 excavations we found additional deeply buried prehistoric materials east of the fort, with a dense layer of 1750s fort artifacts on top of that, and more prehistoric material (which had been pushed outward from the parade ground) on top of that. All of this was, of course, capped with occasional post-1950s artifacts from the modern museum period at the fort. The only way to interpret this pattern of deposition is to conclude that the rebuilding of the fort in the 1950s was accompanied by considerable regrading of the interior of the fort, and that topsoil (and some subsoil) was pushed over the bank to the east. Thus we have prehistoric materials at two different levels in what appears to be a classic case of reverse stratigraphy.

2.3. Stanley Gifford exposing a cache of prehistoric blades. Fort William Henry Museum.

The Prehistory of Fort William Henry

It is often debated whether Native American settlements were only seasonal on Lake George and throughout the Adirondacks, or whether local resources were rich enough to support a more permanent population. Clearly hunting, fishing, and gathering would have been adequate during the warmer months of the year, but without horticulture it is doubtful that year-round villages could have sustained themselves in a forest environment of pine and spruce.

Archeologists working in the Northeastern United States have divided the Native American occupation into the following periods:

Paleo-Indian (circa 9500–8000 B.C.)
Early Archaic (circa 8000–6000 B.C.)
Middle Archaic (circa 6000–4000 B.C.)
Late Archaic (circa 4000–1000 B.C.)
Early Woodland (circa 1000–200 B.C.)
Middle Woodland (circa 200 B.C.–A.D. 1000)
Late Woodland (circa A.D. 1000–1500)

Each of these periods has been fixed in time using radiocarbon dating, and the sequence ends with the Contact Period, as Europeans began moving into the region.

Although fieldwork at Lake George has not been very comprehensive, it has included excavations by Dr. Robert Funk at several sites in the 1960s, including a collaborative effort with Tom and Paul Weinman at the Weinman site on Assembly Point, where archeologists uncovered Late Archaic and late Middle Woodland artifacts between 1963 and 1966 (Funk 1976). Also, in the late 1970s, Dr. Dean Snow dug at the nearby Harrisena site and found an Early Archaic assemblage of bifurcate-base projectile points, Plano and Kirk points, and knives and scrapers, most of which had been manufactured from quartz and quartzite (Snow 1977, 1980). Other sites have been located by amateur archeologists and professionals during the course of cultural resource management surveys. Lake George is thus an area that is reasonably well known for its prehistoric settlements, even though past work has resulted in relatively few publications.

Past research has demonstrated that there are few traces of Paleo-Indians at Lake George — that is, no fluted Clovis points, channel flakes, or scrapers typical of that period have been found in the area. There is little evidence of human occupation there during the Middle Archaic Period, but this rapidly changed during the Late Archaic, when the population was clearly increasing. New styles of projectile points at the fort, typical of the Late Archaic, include the types known as Otter Creek, Vosburg, Lamoka, Brewerton, and Snook Kill. For the entire Archaic Period, hunting and fishing would have been important, along with the gathering of wild plant foods, and by the end of the Archaic, Native Americans' awareness of seasonality and the availability of local resources was no doubt extremely high.

During the next major period — the Woodland — pottery, horticulture, and a more settled lifestyle appeared in the region for the first time. There is little evidence of human occupation in the Early Woodland in the Lake George area, but the Middle and Late Woodland are both well represented in archeological finds, with a wide range of pottery styles, pendants, and the projectile point types known as Jack's Reef and Levanna. The Middle Woodland is especially well represented at Fort William Henry, both in terms of sizable features of fire-cracked rock (see below) and abundant pottery types. This is the one time period for which it could be argued that a relatively permanent village may have been located on the terrace where Fort William Henry was later constructed.

Archeological evidence recovered at Fort William Henry thus suggests a pattern of thousands of years of occupation prior to the arrival of French and British armies. Prehistoric artifacts recovered from the grounds of the fort in the 1950s include large numbers of projectile points (a comprehensive list includes the types known as bifurcate-base, Vosburg, Brewerton, Side-Notched, Jack's Reef Corner-Notched, Jack's Reef Pentagonal, Snook Kill, Orient Fishtail, Levanna, and Madison), bifaces, scrapers, perforators, and worked flakes, as well as very large numbers of pottery sherds.

One of the most time-diagnostic and interesting archeological finds before the reconstruction of Fort William Henry in the 1950s was a small pocket of burned bone from a human cremation burial covered with red ochre (powdered hematite) (Gifford 1955, 7). Associated with this was a ground slate point, suggesting that the grave belonged to the Middlesex Culture of the Early Woodland Period (Ritchie 1980). Other projectile points and bones were found by Carleton Dunn inside what is now the north end of the reconstructed East Barracks (Dunn, personal communication, July 19, 2012). Dr. William Ritchie, then the New York State Archaeologist, was called in to excavate that site and found, among other remains, a Native American skeleton.

Recent Findings

During our recent archeological work at the fort, we have found time-diagnostic stone tools under the West Barracks (fig. 2.4), at the north end of the parade ground (fig. 2.5), and in the dumps east of the fort (figs. 2.6 and 2.7). We have also uncovered two prehistoric fireplaces that were still intact underneath the parade ground. Much more dramatically, in the summer of 1998 we discovered what is commonly termed a roasting platform that was deeply buried outside the east wall of Fort William Henry. North American archeologists define a "roasting platform" as a large cluster of fire-cracked rocks that were most likely used for the processing (smoking, cooking, or drying) of fish; when dated, these platforms typically fall into the Middle Woodland Period. They are most frequently found near rivers and other bodies of water.

The platform we excavated in 1998 was some 1.80 m (6 ft) deep and composed of hundreds of fire-cracked rocks (fig. 2.8). Measuring 2.1 × 1.6 m (6.9 × 5.25 ft), this giant platform was probably used for processing fish caught in Lake George. It would have taken only a minute to walk up from the shore to the sandy terrace above the lake, carrying the day's catch, and put the fish on the platform to be cooked, dried, or smoked. The stones from this feature are currently stored inside the southeast bastion of the fort, awaiting their eventual inclusion in a display for visitors.

In 2012 we exposed another roasting platform, this one east of the fort and within ten meters of the first, proving yet again that Lake George — and especially this terrace overlooking the southern end of the lake — was an ideal location for Native American settlements and food processing (fig. 2.9).

2.4. Examples of prehistoric artifacts excavated from the West Barracks in 1999 and 2000. *Top row:* Jack's Reef Corner-Notched points of chert. *Bottom row, left to right:* bifurcate-base point of rhyolite; Vosburg point of chert; Brewerton Side-Notched point of chert. Far right: quartzite biface.

2.5. Examples of prehistoric stone tools excavated from the north end of the parade ground between 1997 and 2000. *Top row, left to right:* Jack's Reef Pentagonal point of chert; Orient Fishtail point of chert; untyped point of chert. *Bottom row:* untyped chert points.

2.6. Examples of prehistoric artifacts excavated from the dump outside the East Curtain Wall between 1997 and 1999. *Top row, left to right:* Levanna point of chert; Levanna point of chert; Madison point of chert; Levanna point of chert; perforator of chert; perforator of quartzite. *Middle row, left to right:* Jack's Reef Corner-Notched point of jasper; untyped point; Snook Kill point of chert; Snook Kill point of chert. *Bottom row:* two-hole slate gorget fragment (Middle Woodland).

2.7. Examples of prehistoric artifacts excavated from the dump outside the East Curtain Wall in 2011 and 2012. *Top row:* Pottery sherds with cord impressions. *Bottom row, left to right:* clay smoking pipe; clay smoking pipe; Jack's Reef Corner-Notched point of chert; Jack's Reef Corner-Notched point of chert; perforator of chert.

Roasting platforms were probably just one of several specialized adaptations to food gathering on the shores of this Adirondack lake, and they suggest occupations that may have been of some duration. This latest discovery was left *in situ* and was reburied just as it was found, since we recognized that in time it could become a fascinating outdoor exhibit.

The roasting platform we exposed in 2012 measured 2 m (6.56 ft) east-west by a minimum of 1.27 m (4.17 ft) north-south, and its surface lies between 1.05 and 1.15 m (3.44–3.77 ft) below the modern ground surface. Recent historical artifacts extended down to almost the surface of the platform, and we found no artifacts between the stones that might help in dating the platform. However, cord-wrapped sherds found in adjacent test pits suggest that this feature dates to the Middle Woodland Period.

One additional find that is significant, but difficult to interpret, is a single shell bead (wampum) that was found at the northern end of the parade ground in 1997 (fig. 2.10). Was it drilled in prehistoric times, or was it manufactured for trade to Native Americans during the Contact Period? Perhaps it belonged to an Indian who served on the British or the French side during the siege in 1757. Because there is only one, and that is rather crudely made, it is truly an enigma!

2.8. (*Above*) The large roasting platform of fire-cracked rocks discovered in 1998 outside the East Curtain Wall (facing northwest).

2.9. The roasting platform discovered in 2012 outside the East Curtain Wall. The arrow points north, and the vertical rod is marked in 10-cm units.

2.10. A shell bead (wampum) discovered in the parade ground in 1997. The inside diameter is 3.0 mm (0.117 in), and the maximum outside diameter is 8.38 mm (0.33 in).

Native American Pottery at the Fort

Of special significance at Fort William Henry are the great quantities of prehistoric pottery sherds that are found almost everywhere, which represent the remains of dozens of storage pots that were most likely made by women. When pottery was being discovered here in the 1950s, the lead archeologist was greatly impressed by the Middle Woodland occupation, and he mentioned "literally bushels of finely made and decorated pottery" (Gifford 1955, 7). Most of the pottery was discovered in the dump areas east of the fort, but some extensive scatterings from smashed pots were found in 1998 at the north end of the parade ground, just below the modern surface. There large numbers of pottery sherds were splayed across what once had been the surface.

Dr. Victoria Bunker has recently examined many of the more diagnostic pottery sherds from the most recent work at Fort William Henry. Based on her observations, probably none of the sherds is from the Early Woodland Period, as we have found no Vinette 1 pottery, which is considered to be the hallmark of that period. The majority of the pottery is from the Middle Woodland Period, as evidenced by much cord-impressed pottery, linear dentate decoration, some thumbnail decoration, and small circular punctate decoration (figs. 2.11, 2.12, 2.13). Evidence for human presence in the subsequent Late Woodland Period is minor in comparison, and it is represented by a very small amount of incised decoration on pots and by the presence of collared vessels.

Overall Significance

Most of the Native American artifacts excavated at Fort William Henry were no doubt left behind by hunters and gatherers (and fishermen) who were short-term visitors to Lake George, and the archeological finds could easily reflect hundreds or even thousands of brief camps created over a span of 10,000 years. However, the combination of roasting platforms and numerous pottery storage vessels strongly suggests that a substantial Middle Woodland village may have been constructed on this terrace overlooking the lake. This is an exciting prospect, and further work is recommended to determine whether Fort William Henry was constructed squarely on top of a large village of that earlier time period.

However, it does not appear that the Lake George area, or specifically the property where Fort William Henry is located, ever had very much potential for truly permanent villages. Corn arrived in southern portions of New York State in the Middle and Late Woodland Period (Hart and Rieth 2002),

2.11. Pottery excavated at the north end of the parade ground. *Top left:* rim sherd with multiple tool applications; incised rim and small circular punctations; cord impressions angled across lip. *Top right:* rim sherd with cord impressions. *Bottom:* sherd with small circular punctations.

2.12. Pottery sherds with cord impressions (typical Middle Woodland).

2.13. Examples of pottery sherds from the dump outside the East Curtain Wall. *Top row, left to right:* slightly burnished rim sherd with multiple tool applications, chevrons superimposed on horizontal lines, stamping at lip and incisions; cord-impressed rim sherd with punctations done from exterior (several go all the way through); rim sherd with cord impressions. *Bottom row, left to right:* sherd with angles and triangle incised over horizontal; sherd with thumbnail decoration; sherd with cord impressions.

but its growing season would have been too long for it to adapt quickly to Lake George and the surrounding areas in the Adirondacks. Lake George was clearly a superb area for fishing and hunting, but without horticulture, it would have remained chiefly a hunting territory that was used by Indians living around its perimeter.

The Reconstruction of
the Fort in the 1950s

CARLETON DUNN (fig. 3.1) was twenty years old when he was hired in 1953 by the team that was rebuilding Fort William Henry. He had often worked as a lifeguard on the beach below, where he had found several shipwrecks, but now he was allowed to dig inside the fort in the ruins of both the South Barracks and the East Barracks (Dunn, personal communication, July 19, 2012). He even was called in to identify the human bones found below the south end of the East Barracks (see chapter 6), the spot later identified as "the crypt." Thus began this passionate visitor's lifelong love for the historic fort, and variations on this story have no doubt been repeated thousands of times by other visitors. About 60,000 tourists viewed the dig site each summer in the 1950s (fig. 3.2). They watched the fort literally being rebuilt from the ashes (fig. 3.3), and a great many of these visitors are still returning today, accompanied by their children and grandchildren. The story of Fort William Henry is undeniably just as relevant and fascinating for today's visitors, each of whom will no doubt carry away their own stories, perhaps about the kindness of an interpreter or the distinctiveness of an artifact in one of the exhibit cases.

Ironically, the reconstruction of the fort almost did not happen because the property was going to be bulldozed in the 1950s, to make way for a train station. Luckily a group of local business people stepped in and decided to rebuild the fort as a commercial tourist attraction. It was in an excellent setting because the Lake George area was immensely popular with tourists. The first Fort William Henry Hotel had been built nearby in 1855, and trolley lines subsequently reached the area from Poughkeepsie. Visitors arrived in carriages and then in automobiles, and in 1872 the site of Fort William Henry was sold to the Lake Champlain Transportation Company, which was later affiliated with the Delaware and Hudson Railroad Company.

The first Fort William Henry Hotel burned down in 1870; it was replaced in the following year, and then the replacement burned in 1908. Its successor, according to Robert Flacke Sr., long-term CEO of the Fort William Henry Corporation, was in 1911 "the first fireproof hotel in the United States" (personal communication, July 15, 2011). Business dropped off during the

3.1. (*Right*) Carleton Dunn in 2012, speaking to the archeology team inside the cemetery building. Carleton has been a superb bridge between the digs of the 1950s and those of the present, helping us better understand the challenges and excitement of the original excavations at the fort.

3.2. (*Below*) Postcard view of "FORT WILLIAM HENRY, Lake George, N.Y. Looking north over the Fort showing its strategic location at the head of Lake George. Built in 1755 by Sir William Johnson, North American Agent for King George, much bloody action took place between the French, British and their Indian Allies before the Fort fell to General Marquis de Montcalm in 1757." Color photo by Richard K. Dean.

Great Depression, and the site of the fort began to go downhill when the Delaware and Hudson was broken up by President Theodore Roosevelt, the trust buster. With the Lake George area in decline, the land was sold for just $50,000 during World War II, and it clearly would take an inspired vision to turn this situation around.

Fortunately, late in 1952 the Fort William Henry Corporation was formed by area business people who bought the nineteen-acre property, including the hotel. Harold G. Veeder, Alden Shaw, Horace Van Voast Jr., Harold Blodgett, John Wendell, E. J. McEnaney, and William Gilmour were central to this effort, and a major part of their business plan was to construct a replica of the original fort about 300 feet east of the Fort William Henry Hotel. A newspaper article at that time noted that "today all that remains are the depressions and general outline — a square with diamond-shaped protuberances jutting from each corner" (Ft. Wm. Henry to Be Rebuilt" 1952). The fort site was covered with tall pine trees, but there was little on the surface to suggest what might lie beneath (fig. 3.4). Visitors to each consecutive Fort William Henry Hotel often walked over the ruins, and there was endless speculation about whether bodies lay buried there.

Archeology was necessary from the very beginning because the new corporation needed to determine the footprint of the original fort, and extensive excavations would be required to supplement the original British engineers' drawings. The corporation's directors also wanted to recover original artifacts that would help in the creation of exciting new exhibits. Professional archeology had rarely been used in the reconstruction of local forts prior to this time, although artifacts were occasionally collected from the surface or excavated from military sites in the region (Calver and Bolton 1950; Starbuck 1999a). Only at National Park Service sites and a few larger private sites such as Colonial Williamsburg was historical archeology systematically being used as an expected part of the reconstruction process.

3.4. Postcard view of "LAKE GEORGE, N.Y. WEST DITCH OF OLD FORT WM. HENRY."

3.5. Stanley Gifford examining a stone ax, possibly comparing it to European axes of the 1750s that are lying on the table in front of him. Note his tobacco pipe and plaid tie, which are not common fixtures among archeologists today!

Stanley Gifford, an experienced archeologist who had worked at other historic and prehistoric sites (fig. 3.5), was hired in 1953 and placed in charge of locating the outlines of key buildings, the original ground level, and the military cemetery. (The cemetery's location was not marked on any historical plans of the property.) He was assisted by his wife, Ruth, and by college students who completely excavated the northwest bastion of the fort, where the French bombardment had been most pronounced. Almost predictably, nearly all newspaper accounts from Gifford's day claimed that the French had stacked the bodies of the defenders of the fort into an enormous pile in the middle of the fort and then created a huge funeral pyre. There was no

3.6. (*Top left*) An intact mortar shell discovered in 1955 is being deactivated by the 542nd Ordnance Detachment, Explosive Ordnance Disposal Control. The shell was still filled with black powder. Fort William Henry Museum.

3.7. (*Top right*) Artifacts found at the north end of the East Barracks, believed to come from the remains of a blacksmith shop. *Times-Union* (Albany, NY), August 29, 1954. Fort William Henry Museum.

3.8. (*Left*) An English mortar shell with a human scalp attached to it. This was found in the foundation of one of the barracks buildings in October 1954. Was this scalp, with its black hair, ripped from the head of a defender of the fort? Fort William Henry Museum.

merit to the story, and it may be argued that one of Gifford's biggest tasks was to combat the sensationalistic myths that had grown up around the fort.

Gifford typically dug where structures were about to be rebuilt, and much of the dirt excavated by his crew was dumped into a giant, motorized sifting machine at the southwest corner of the parade ground. They found fragments of mortar shells and even one intact shell (fig. 3.6), dozens of cannonballs, hundreds of flattened musket balls, buckshot, axes, pewter spoons, knives, tobacco pipes, canteens, and much, much more in the charred ruins. Human remains were sometimes recovered (see chapter 6), and tools that might have come from a blacksmith shop were found under the northern end of the East Barracks (fig. 3.7). Unquestionably the most unusual find was a human scalp with black hair that was stuck to the side of a still-intact mortar shell (fig. 3.8).

3.9. A "new" Fort William Henry is rising from the ashes in the early 1950s. Fort William Henry Museum.

3.10. Oxen were used to drag the timbers of the new fort into place. Fort William Henry Museum.

Sometimes the original British plans located buildings in different positions from where archeology showed them to have been; in other cases the British plans had been followed more closely (Carleton Dunn, personal communication, July 19, 2012). This meant that some reconstructed buildings were as much as eight or ten feet away from the original foundations. Although these deviations might cause some to question the accuracy of the reconstruction, they proved to be unexpectedly positive because they left the foundations of the West Barracks and East Barracks relatively intact and available for future archeology.

Gifford ultimately recovered tens of thousands of artifacts, although that may not be what he is best known for. Most archeologists are "characters,"

3.11. An aerial view of Fort William Henry as it was reconstructed. Fort William Henry Museum.

and "Stan" was no exception. Hard-drinking and feisty, he wore an Indiana Jones–style felt hat and khakis, always had his trademark pipe hanging from one corner of his mouth, and carried a .38. Sadly, Stan died in 1961 without writing a final excavation report.

As Stan wrapped up his work in 1954, Canadian loggers brought in timber, and new log walls were quickly put up (figs. 3.9, 3.10), guided by the archeological finds and by the eighteenth-century engineers' drawings of the fort (Gifford 1955). The northwest bastion was rebuilt with steel, and the other three bastions were rebuilt as wooden box-and-beam structures (fig. 3.11). Jack Binder, a superb artist (see appendix 1), designed highly realistic mannequins to go in the displays (figs. 3.12, 3.13), and the reconstructed fort opened in 1955, with a great many original artifacts on display. Although even today entertaining stories are told about Stan's colorful activities at the fort, his excavation records have never been found, leading some to suggest that all of his papers must have been destroyed when a fire set by an arsonist burned the reconstructed West Barracks in 1967. Numerous artifacts recovered in the 1950s were also destroyed in that fire, and new exhibits had to be created to fill that building.

Since the 1950s the exhibits and tours at Fort William Henry have steadily evolved. The fort is very popular with school groups every spring and campers every summer, and it is viewed as an extremely family-friendly way to learn more about the French and Indian War. In the popular resort community of Lake George, it is easily one of the best attractions.

It was not until the 1990s that archeology resumed here under the auspices of Adirondack Community College (now the State University of New

3.12. A medical exhibit on the second floor of the North Barracks. This always popular topic is tempered by the fact that effective medicines were rare, and amputation was the "cure" for a great many injuries.

3.13. This exhibit in the North Barracks shows Colonel George Monro seated at his table and preparing to write with a quill pen.

3.14. Marching into the parade ground to greet the public in 2012. Dan Donahue, chief interpreter, is in the lead.

York Adirondack), and below-ground research since then has been accompanied by new exhibits, spirited military demonstrations, and evening ghost tours inside the fort. The ghost tours in particular (called the "Spirits of History Tour") have been a popular and commercial success and have been featured on the program *Ghost Hunters* on television's Syfy channel.

Fort William Henry continues to be a very exciting place to visit, and its greatest assets are that it has truly wonderful stories to tell and dedicated staff members who are proud to honor the British soldiers who served here (fig. 3.14). It is by no means easy to keep up with the changing expectations of modern visitors, especially given the cost of the latest interactive technology, but solid story lines are central to the recreated fort's success.

The 1990s

Archeology inside Barracks, Dumps, and a Well

IT WAS THE SUMMER of 1997, and I was crouched inside the fort's well (fig. 4.1). Much, much earlier, in 1756, Rogers's Rangers had dug this stone-lined well, and it had never provided enough water. Now I had descended into the well, hoping to find artifacts from the time period of the fort and maybe even the remains of a massacre victim or two. Twenty feet above me (fig.4.2), I could hear the sounds of my students and colleagues in the parade ground as they dug into the remains of barracks buildings and dumps. I completed the excavation of the well in that one summer, but for four summers we dug in a host of locations, seeking evidence of what life must have been like inside Fort William Henry more than 250 years ago.

Our arrival at Fort William Henry to conduct research in the late 1990s was really a by-product of the forensic archeology that had been conducted in the military cemetery outside the fort in 1993 and 1995 (see chapter 6). It was after that very exciting research that I was approached by Michael Palumbo, then the curator of Fort William Henry, who told me that the owners of the fort were eager to host a new series of archeological investigations. This led to excavations over the next four years, from 1997 to 2000, as I directed summer field schools from Adirondack Community College both inside and outside the reconstructed fort. We often had seventy or more volunteers and college students digging with us each summer, all of whom were eager to participate in original research at such a remarkable site.

Public education was an enormous part of our research effort because up to four thousand tourists a day walked through the reconstructed fort. Most of them knew very little about the French and Indian War, few had ever seen a dig before, and all were eager to fire questions at us for hours. Of course, virtually all said that they wished they were digging with us. Archeology is a powerful tool for learning about the past, and with American schools teaching less and less about the colonial wars, it was rather humbling to re- alize that the five or ten minutes spent talking with our diggers might be a visitor's best adult exposure to "our" war, "our" fort, and "our" archeological methods.

4.1. The surface of the fort's 1756 well, blocked off for security reasons while the excavation was underway in 1997. The hoist was used to lift countless buckets of dirt out of the well, as well as the archeologist who was digging inside.

4.2. Looking up the culvert that was installed inside the 1756 well. Gerald Bradfield, then the curator of Fort William Henry, is peering down from the top of the culvert. In the center of the picture is the hose that ran upward from a submersible pump that kept the well "reasonably" comfortable at the bottom.

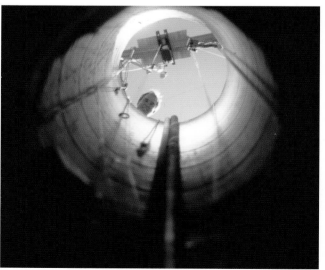

Excavation Areas

THE WELL

Our research inside the fort opened up sizable parts of the parade ground, where we sometimes descended for eight feet or more inside the cellars of former barracks buildings. One of the most significant features that we excavated was the original well for the fort, located at the north end of the parade ground. In all of the years after the fort was destroyed, the top of the well had jutted out from the ruins, and since about 1955, tourists had thrown their own "artifacts" into the well, ranging from flash cubes to wads of chewing gum, plastic toys, and sunglasses (Starbuck 2001). For eighteenth-century soldiers, it had been their only source of water during the French siege; for twentieth-century tourists, it was a wishing well; and for modern archeologists, it was a thirty-foot-deep time capsule that showed the changing history of Lake George.

We erected an electric hoist and a wood crossbeam above the well, inserted a steel culvert into the upper part of the shaft (fig. 4.3), and started digging down through the "recent" artifacts. Close to the surface were hundreds of pounds of pennies thrown in by modern visitors. Deeper layers in the well represented the many years that the well had stood open after the destruction of the fort, and deeper still were artifacts from the 1750s, including lead musket balls, French gunflints, fragments of tobacco pipes, and many small pieces of cut lead that may have been hem weights (fig. 4.4). All of these had been dropped into the well and were lost until I climbed inside it and began sending its contents out in buckets. For the entire time I was in the well, a video camera was positioned inside the culvert, recording and broadcasting my every move to two television monitors so that visitors could "participate" in the research.

Toward the bottom, beginning at a depth of about twenty-seven feet, was the top of an oval barrel lining that had holes drilled through the wood, permitting groundwater to enter the well (figs. 4.5, 4.6). The boards were each three inches thick and six to twelve inches wide, and the diameter of the opening at the bottom of the well varied between thirty and thirty-five inches. Today groundwater begins to flow into the well at a depth of about twenty-three and a half feet below the modern surface, and I reached a maximum depth of nearly thirty feet before I finally had to halt for safety reasons. Attaining that depth required a submersible pump, and I still had not reached the bottom of the wood lining. There were compensating factors, though, because it was a constant fifty-two degrees inside the well, which made it a very pleasant place to spend the summer. My students, in contrast, were sweating up above on the parade ground and probably feeling rather envious.

4.3. (*Above*) Inserting a section of culvert into the fort's well, just before the excavation began in 1997.

4.4. (*Right*) Examples of artifacts found at the bottom of the well, between twenty-seven and twenty-nine feet below the current surface. The artifacts include French gunflints, musket balls, pieces of cut lead, tobacco pipe fragments, and an iron ring that encircled the base of a post or a tent peg.

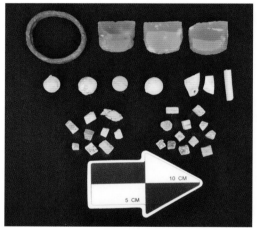

We returned that fall in a final effort to reach the bottom of the well, and we worked until September 25, 1997, when safety concerns finally forced me to stop. Probing revealed that the barrel lining of the well was at least five feet nine inches in height, and I never did reach the absolute bottom. On the very last day, my field notes give a sense of just how risky the well dig had become:

> As I pulled out the larger stones in the bottom, I realized that I was creating sink holes. In effect, quicksand was making it hard to stand: I kept sinking 6–8" in more and more spots, and the pump was also sinking up to 4" in the sand. There no longer was a solid bottom. The last straw was not the constant rain of sand and stones from above, although that worried me. The culvert gave

4.5. (*Above*) The barrel lining at the bottom of the 1756 well. This photograph shows just the tops of the boards, which extended down several additional feet.

4.6. (*Left*) A close-up of water pouring through an opening drilled in the lining of the well.

some protection, but lots of stones were still shooting down onto me. Rather, at about 3:30 I realized that the ground water coming in was now about 50 percent sand — brown, and it was filling in the well. I was losing more ground, and a big collapse could be the only outcome. I asked Gerry [Bradfield] to hoist me out. When I got to the surface of the well at 4:00, I saw that all around the top of the well it had sunk another 8–10" just today!! The well was sinking much faster than at any time in July. Our pump worked better, we were moving dirt much quicker, and therefore the whole well shaft was sinking much faster. A hopeless situation. The artifacts that came out today we bagged as "28–29 feet." We found three more musket balls, several tiny pieces of lead, one French gunflint, one corner of a case bottle, one small sherd of delftware (tin-glazed earthenware), many tiny animal bones, and one iron ring (2" diameter). We also had lots of recent tourist artifacts mixed in, right down to the very bottom of the well.

A huge question remains. How was the well originally dug? Did Rangers risk their lives digging down through soft sand for thirty feet or more? The best answer may be that of Joe McEvoy of the New York State Office of Parks, Recreation and Historic Preservation (personal communication, October 23, 1997). His interpretation is that the well may have begun as a hole that was dug ten feet in diameter at ground level. The Rangers would have immediately put in about six feet of vertical planks (oak or elm) so they would always be surrounded by the "barrel" as they descended. They would have put a wood curb underneath the vertical planks and then started adding stones on top of the planks. The weight of the stones pressing down on the planks would have helped to force the lining down as they dug out from underneath the curb. This way they never had water washing in on them as they dug. Finally, as they reached the maximum depth, they quickly drilled two or three holes in the wood lining and then climbed up and out of the well as the groundwater began to pour in. No doubt the well could have been dug in other ways, but this approach would probably have been the safest.

THE PARADE GROUND

In 1997 and 1998 we conducted modest excavations in the northeast, northwest, and southeast corners of the parade ground, typically finding that both eighteenth-century and prehistoric artifacts were literally side by side, no more than a foot below the modern surface. We did not try digging in the center of this open space or in the southwest corner because that would have interfered with the flow of visitors and tours through the courtyard. Besides, based on 1950s photographs, it appeared that Stanley Gifford had already disturbed much of this central area, and when our excavations began in the southeast corner of the parade ground in 1997, we discovered old, backfilled trenches everywhere we dug (fig. 4.7).

We were most successful at the northern end of the parade ground and between the well and the previously dug northwest bastion. Here it appeared that regrading and leveling of the parade ground in the 1950s had taken off all dirt down to a point just above where British soldiers had walked. Artifacts of all types were abundant, and it was surface scatter that we were exposing. However, we were more eager to focus on building foundations and what they might contain.

THE WEST BARRACKS

Between 1998 and 2000 our most intensive excavations were inside the foundations of the West Barracks, where we exposed over fifty feet of the burned structure (fig. 4.8). Soil layers appeared heavily disturbed and were full of charcoal (fig. 4.9). We found the stone base of a massive, mortared barracks fireplace that was nine feet on a side (fig. 4.10); we found evidence of small rooms in the cellar (fig. 4.11); and we even found stains from postmolds and burned beams that were running north-south along what had been the east wall of the barracks (fig. 4.12). The artifacts were just as interesting, and we found personal and utilitarian items used by the soldiers and officers during their two years of residence, including buttons, buckles, cuff links, a ring, the stem of a wineglass, delftware medicine cups (fig. 4.13), lead gaming

4.8. (*Top*) Excavating the interior of the West Barracks in 1999 (looking north). From left to right are John Farrell, Matthew Rozell, and Gerald Bradfield.

4.9. (*Middle*) A stratigraphic profile through the interior of the West Barracks (facing northwest). The dark, charcoal-filled layers give a sense of how heavily disturbed the cellar really is, with charcoal, ash, brick, and stone thoroughly inter-mixed. The arrow points north, and the vertical rod is marked in 10-cm units.

4.10. (*Bottom*) The east side of a fireplace base inside the West Barracks. The upper portion of the fireplace appears to have been removed during the 1950s reconstruction. The arrow points north, and the vertical rod is marked in 10-cm units.

4.11. (*Above*) Matthew Rozell is excavating inside a small room in the cellar of the West Barracks. Above this depth (one and a half meters down) the contents of the barracks were heavily disturbed, but at this depth the charred remains of boards were visible on all sides of the room.

4.12. (*Left*) The dark, linear stain in the center is all that is left of the east wall of the West Barracks. The string in the right rear marks the outline of a posthole, with the base of a wood post still standing upright.

pieces, part of a grinding stone (fig. 4.14), the base from a case bottle, the bone inlay from a knife handle, scissors, a brass spoon, and fish hooks. We also found thousands of pieces of animal bones, fragments of mortar shells, cast iron grapeshot and canister shot, lead musket balls, gunflints, and a bayonet fragment. There were even sewing supplies inside the cellar of the barracks, including a thimble, needle, and numerous pins.

4.13. (*Left*) Portions of two delftware medicine cups found inside the West Barracks.

4.14. (*Right*) Part of a grinding stone found inside the West Barracks.

While we were working on the West Barracks, visitors to the fort would often ask us "how accurate" the reconstructed fort is. We would invariably tell them that if the West Barracks had been reconstructed precisely on the footprint of the original foundation, then everything would have been removed or destroyed—there would have been nothing left for us to find. As it was, this building foundation was the most intact site that our team has found at Fort William Henry, and it contains the most evidence from domestic, everyday activities. When we finished in 2000, we left the fireplace and burned timbers intact where we found them and backfilled the cellar. The remains of this structure have tremendous potential for further research.

THE EAST BARRACKS

In 1997 we excavated a trench at the northern end of where the East Barracks had stood (fig. 4.15). Given the large quantities of charcoal and rubble, we were probably very close to where Gifford had found what he thought might be a blacksmith shop. There were bricks and mortar shells here, and burned timbers that were very deep, so it clearly was an interesting site. However, unlike the West Barracks, there was so much disturbance here, down to two meters and more, that we kept our excavations very limited and moved on to other structures. We recognized that it would have required a major effort to expose very much of this site.

THE CEMETERY AREA OUTSIDE THE FORT

We commenced digging next to the Cemetery Building in 1997, hoping to find either skeletons or outbuildings. Unfortunately, this was another area where Gifford had left numerous trenches behind, so we worked there for

4.15. A trench dug at the northeast corner of the parade ground (inside the East Barracks) in the summer of 1997. Children sometimes watched for what seemed like hours, many hoping to become archeologists themselves.

only one season. Some years later, Sarah Majot, the owner of the archeological consulting firm ARCH TECH, directed a public education project here in 2005 and dug several additional pits with a crew of volunteers. Approximately 800 visitors to the fort were guided out to the excavation that summer, where they learned proper excavation and laboratory techniques.

THE MOAT OUTSIDE THE FORT

In 1999 we excavated several pits in the moat just outside the modern (west) entrance to the fort. This had always been a dry moat, and we discovered planks that were three inches thick from a wood walkway that would have spanned the moat. However, based on the associated beer bottles, the walkway probably dated not to the colonial period but to the early twentieth

4.16. (*Left*) A trench in the dump outside the East Curtain Wall of the fort (facing north), with Andrew Farry, a field supervisor, on the left. The sheets of plywood, with cross-bracing, helped shore up the sandy walls, but collapses were still frequent.

4.17. (*Right*) A major trench in 1999 through the dump outside the East Curtain Wall (facing west toward the reconstructed fort).

century. Archeologists have dug moats elsewhere, and they often are good sources of artifacts. That was not the case at Fort William Henry, where we discovered only a few musket balls. Oral history suggests that Gifford may have dug part of the moat, and that could explain why we found so little.

DUMPS

We conducted very extensive trenching outside the eastern wall of the reconstructed fort. The dump that lies on the downhill slope east of the fort is by far the largest known dump on the fort grounds, and it contains virtually all types of garbage, with food remains predominating. Between 1997 and 1999 we dug several trenches into the dump, descending to depths approaching three meters or more below the modern surface. Given the depth of these deposits, some of our trenches almost resembled the step trenches dug by past generations of archeologists working in the Middle East, where a wide trench at the surface was gradually "stepped down" to a very narrow trench at the bottom of the excavation (figs. 4.16, 4.17). Only by digging in this fashion could we prevent the steep side walls from collapsing onto the diggers below. We successfully avoided any major pit collapses, but when I look now at photographs from that time, I realize that we really were very lucky.

In the dump we discovered about 16,000 fragments of butchered bones, especially from cows, pig, and fish (see appendix 2). These were accompanied by seventy-five musket balls, thirty-five British and thirty-two French gunflints, metal buttons, cuff links, buckles, British halfpennies, a Spanish silver real, two mouth harps, and many hundreds of pottery sherds and fragments of wine bottles. (Artifact counts appear in Starbuck 2002.) There had been at least several hundred soldiers living in the fort over a period of two years, and they had walked only a very short distance to dispose of their garbage — everything lay within about thirty feet of the fort's outer wall.

It would have been easy to spend additional years digging in the eastern dump, but by 1999 we recognized that it was better to approach this as preservationists, leaving a reasonable proportion of the dump for future generations of archeologists to dig. Still, we felt that we had been successful in demonstrating that material in this dump dates to the French and Indian War because of the dearth of numbered regimental buttons or pottery types that would date to the American Revolution. There really was nothing there to prove whether or not General Abercromby's army had camped there in 1758 or General Amherst's army in 1759. They may very well have stationed soldiers atop the burned ruins of the fort, but there was no artifact evidence in the dump to conclusively prove that.

Final Thoughts

When our excavations at Fort William Henry came to a halt at the end of the 2000 field season, it was not because we had run out of interesting areas to explore. Research at other sites in Lake George and Fort Edward was starting to pull us in other directions, but we definitely wanted to return to Fort William Henry if given the opportunity. After all, this fort is the basis for some of the most interesting stories of the French and Indian War, the fort is situated in a majestic setting overlooking Lake George, it was a pleasure to work with the staff here, and we were a center of attention for thousands of visitors every day (even if their nonstop questions were causing us to dig rather slowly).

But from a research perspective, our most significant conclusion after four years of excavations was that Gifford had left large areas still waiting to be explored. True, the 1953–54 excavations had disturbed large areas both inside and outside the fort, but the West Barracks was largely untouched, and the dump located east of the fort was also largely intact. We could only wonder what other finds were still waiting to be uncovered if some day we would be able to return to Fort William Henry.

New Archeology at the Fort

2011–12

DO ARCHEOLOGISTS EVER FIND something that is truly unique? There really are times when a lucky find causes us to be absolutely thrilled, surprised, and profoundly curious all at the same time. In the summer of 2011, when one of our field supervisors, Lauren Sheridan, discovered a brass arrowhead in the ruins of the East Barracks at the fort (fig. 5.1), all of these emotions became very real for us. Fort William Henry was a relatively recent site on the frontier, dating well after the first contacts had been made between Europeans and Native Americans. This ordinarily would mean that we should not expect to find artifacts from the early Contact Period — that is, European objects that were traded to Native Americans and modified by them into traditional forms and functions. Yet here was a piece of European brass, perhaps cut from a kettle and reshaped into a triangular arrowhead, and it was the very first brass arrowhead that we had found in twenty years of digging local British military sites from the French and Indian War. This projectile appears to have still been in use when most warriors on the frontier had switched over to European-style weapons. It was an exciting reminder that surprising finds really do occur on archeological digs. It should be noted, however, that Stanley Gifford had also found "Brass arrows" in the ruins of the fort (1955, 8), but like us, he could not determine whether they were from an Indian settlement on the site before the fort was built, or whether they arrived during its 1755–57 occupation by the military, perhaps as arrows shot into the fort.

Overview

After a hiatus of eleven years, we were asked if we would like to return to Fort William Henry to resume our excavations, and in July 2011 we commenced an additional two seasons of exploration under the sponsorship of the State University of New York Adirondack. We dug for six weeks each summer in 2011 and 2012 because we wanted to have a better look at the East Barracks, which we had only lightly tested in 1998, and we wanted a larger artifact sample from the food dump, or midden, that lies just outside

5.1. A brass arrowhead discovered inside the remains of the East Barracks. It was found deeply buried in the rubble inside the barracks, and one corner of the base was severely bent over, as was the tip. It measures 3.2 cm (1.25 in) long.

the eastern wall (called the East Curtain Wall) of the reconstructed fort. Experienced volunteers plus students from several colleges took part each season, and within this very public setting, we were able once again to expose thousands of visitors to archeology and the history of the French and Indian War.

One change from our work in the 1990s was that in 2011 we began giving formal archeological tours to visitors, offered three times each day by a full-time guide, Dale Erhardt. We also advertised lunchtime archeology lectures to visitors on every day we worked, and we spent more time conversing with the lay public than ever before. Given our ever-increasing contact with visitors, we became more aware of some of the reasons why people choose to visit this frontier fort and, with a touch of irony, we noticed that the Canadian visitors to the fort tended to ask the best questions. They frequently knew much more about our colonial history than did our American visitors. Still, Americans who came to our dig could be quite entertaining — without meaning to be. On July 13, 2011, for example, a small boy walked up to one of our pits and asked, "Are you digging up bugs?" On July 22 another visitor asked, "Are you digging for worms?" And, somewhat embarrassingly, on July 26 a man said to his companion, "Look, dear, at the actors pretending to be archeologists." Archeology can be very humbling sometimes.

The East Barracks

In both 2011 and 2012, we excavated a large block of pits under the northern end of the East Barracks, which runs north-south on the eastern side of the parade ground. Portions of this large foundation had been excavated in the 1950s, and at that time skeletons had been discovered within the so-called crypt close to the south end of the building (fig. 5.2). At the north end, Gifford's team found tools they believed had come from a blacksmith shop (fig. 5.3), but no drawings survived showing exactly where these features had been excavated, and it really was an enormous, largely undocumented structure. Still, news reports from Gifford's day gave a sense of how important this building is:

5.2. A view of the 1957 excavation into the south end of the East Barracks, revealing just how thoroughly the foundation was disturbed. Fort William Henry Museum.

What is believed to be the blacksmith shop of Fort William Henry was located by staff archeologists yesterday. . . . Found after an archeologist's shovel went one foot deeper into the East Barracks area, were nine hewing axes, a Rogers Rangers tomahawk, a 24-pound cannon ball, a shovel, heavy iron bar of the type used as cannon axles, a copper lead ladle for bullet making, and several finished pieces of iron work used on the cannon and cannon cartridges. . . . The East Barracks diggings also have uncovered much of the log work left after the massacre and burning in 1757. Some of the logs at the base of the fortification were charred only on the outside, were solid inside." ("Archeologists Find Blacksmith Shop" 1954)

In 1997 our own team had excavated a single trench close to the northern end of this foundation but found disturbed stratigraphy for at least the one and a half meters (fig. 5.4) (Starbuck 2002, 41).

Our 2011 excavations were meant to help us more fully understand what had survived from this building, and we began excavating three pits, each one by two meters. As we dug down, we truly were descending through "shifting sand" as we sought the footings of the building. What this no doubt meant was that much of the interior of the East Barracks had been

excavated with power equipment in the 1950s, and then the loose dirt had been pushed back into the cellar. Our trench walls were soft and crumbly and always in danger of collapsing. As we proceeded down through the first one and a half meters, we found recent aluminum foil, an aluminum pie plate, and Coke bottle fragments, all suggesting a great deal of disturbance in the 1950s. Also, with such loose soil, our trench walls caved in every time it rained. Interestingly enough, as we descended into the deeper, charcoal-filled layers of the cellar, we found great chunks of melted cinders (fig. 5.5), and these tended to confirm the blacksmith shop hypothesis that had originally been suggested in the 1950s. After scraping through many pockets of disturbed soil at the top of the East Barracks foundation, we finally reached undisturbed black layers from the 1750s, where all of the artifacts reflected the final conflagration at the fort (fig. 5.6). It was here that we found the brass arrowhead, along with many burned artifacts.

SOME FIELD NOTES

A short entry from my 2011 field notes gives a sense of what it was like to dig through this confusing jumble of soil layers:

> Layer 1 is the crushed rock on top of the parade ground.
> Layer 2 is yellow sand that must be Gifford's backdirt from the 1950s.
> Layer 3 is dark brown earth. The upper part of this includes some 1950s material, such as aluminum foil and film wrappers; the lower part of the layer is

5.4. (*Left*) Our previous (1997) excavation into the cellar of the East Barracks. Note that the archeological team is about a foot into the more intact, charcoal-filled bottom of the foundation.

5.5. (*Below*) One of many hardened chunks of melted cinders, or slag, found at the northern end of the East Barracks. This evidence of extreme heat may suggest the presence of a smithy, although the final conflagration that leveled the fort may also have produced furnace-like temperatures.

5.6. Soil layers at the northern end of the East Barracks. The shallower, brown earth reflects recent backfill, while the deeper black layer contains period artifacts from the 1750s.

5.7. Large, scattered stones from an East Barracks fireplace, facing north.

dark with charcoal and uncontaminated by recent artifacts. This deepest part is all 1750s and contains much burnt debris, plus many nails, pieces of lead sprue, tobacco pipes, one silver Spanish real, metal buttons, and finally a mortar bomb fragment at 2.305 m deep. We dug to a depth of 2.44 m below ground surface, but only within a modest trench. We had so many cave-ins of the walls that for the last week we spent half of each day just cleaning up collapse. We dug through a huge amount of backfill to get to the [earth] floor of the barracks. On the north side of the trench we found a massive pile of stones that were totally encrusted with mortar. This must be what has survived from a barracks fireplace.

A BARRACKS FIREPLACE

In 2011 we found the side of a large barracks fireplace base that we continued to expose in 2012 (fig. 5.7). The surface of the fireplace begins about 1.60 m below ground surface, and although it was clearly disturbed in the 1950s, once it is stabilized, this fireplace has the potential to become a fascinating outdoor exhibit. We did not initially realize it was a fireplace, but the stones bear a strong resemblance to a much more intact fireplace that rests in the cellar of the reconstructed West Barracks (fig. 5.8). Our 2012 excavation also revealed that the East Barracks contains numerous fragments of exploded mortar bombs (fig. 5.9), grapeshot, and musket balls, most likely a result of the final bombardment by the French in 1757. And everywhere there were melted lumps of lead from casting musket balls, many more than we had found anywhere else in the fort (see table 5.1).

5.8. (*Above*) The barracks fireplace that has survived underneath the reconstructed West Barracks. It is mortared and remarkably intact.

5.9. (*Left*) Fragments of mortar shells discovered inside the foundation of the East Barracks.

A CAVE-IN

We moved and sifted great quantities of earth from within the East Barracks. One day in 2011 a tour group was passing by our excavation, and a woman pointed across the open trench and asked, "What is that round object?" And sure enough, there was a rather roundish object in the far wall (probably a stone). One of our diggers walked up to it with his finger extended, and just before he touched it, the entire three-meter-high wall collapsed into the bottom of the trench. The tourist was mortified, clearly believing that her request had led to the disastrous collapse. For the remainder of her tour, I could see her casting furtive glances in our direction — she was no doubt afraid that we were about to exact revenge on her for apparently destroying our excavation. She never did learn that the "object" in the wall had never even been touched. In fact, the wall had collapsed because one of our diggers had been sitting too close to the edge of the excavation.

TABLE 5.1. Artifacts Recovered from Fort William Henry, 2011–12		
Artifacts	East Barracks	East Curtain Wall Dump
ARMAMENTS		
Musket balls (complete)	19	18
Musket balls (flattened)	2	1
Musket balls (chewed)	2	
Musket ball (cut in quarters)		1
Small lead shot (buckshot)	6	19
Lead slag	153	9
Grapeshot	7	4
Canister shot		3
Mortar shell fragments	8	4
Gunflints, British	2	6
Gunflints, French	8	8
Gunflint fragments, French	4	5
Gunflints, burned	4	4
Lead gunflint patch	1	
Brass arrowhead	1	
UTILITARIAN		
Lead weight		1
Cut lead (hem weights)	53	
Ox shoe	1	
CUTLERY		
Knife with bone handle		1
Knife with wood handle	1	
GLASS		
Table glass fragments		24
Wine bottle fragments	129	158
Medicine bottle fragments	2	2
Case bottle fragments	2	2
SEWING EQUIPMENT		
Brass pin		1
Handle from large shears		1

TABLE 5.1. (*Continued*)		
Artifacts	East Barracks	East Curtain Wall Dump
PERSONAL ADORNMENTS		
Buttons, metal	7	1
Buttons, bone		1
Cuff links		1
Buckle fragments	1	3
TOBACCO PIPES		
Stem fragments	49	81
Bowl fragments	16	
COINS		
British farthing (1749)		2
Spanish one-half real (1751)	1	

We had experienced several cave-ins of our pit walls in 2011, and when we returned to the fort in 2012 the maintenance crew was immensely helpful in shoring up the vertical walls of our trenches to better protect our diggers in the bottom of the trenches. In 2012 we opened up an area five meters by five meters and excavated it as a single unit in order to expose a large expanse around the barracks fireplace (fig. 5.10). As the excavation proceeded, period artifacts and charcoal were found all over the surface of the fireplace. But more important, this was clearly not a barracks fireplace that was solely used for heating and cooking. This fireplace was the centerpiece of activities that had produced a great deal of melted lead sprue (from casting musket balls). Small, cut pieces of lead — which might be hem weights — were abundant here (fig. 5.11); there were large, melted cinders that suggested prolonged periods of intense heat; and musket balls, grapeshot, and chunks of burned wood were scattered everywhere (fig. 5.12). With so much activity here, it really does appear to be our team's first evidence for a maintenance or processing area within the fort, and it adds great credibility to the interpretation that this was the fireplace for a blacksmith shop.

We also succeeded in reaching burned boards at the very bottom of the eastern wall of the East Barracks (fig. 5.13), and glacial sand lay underneath. This was approximately ten feet below the modern surface, but we did not remove any of the boards. (This very deep trench would have to be expanded considerably before any of the boards could be removed safely.) A truly exciting discovery was made on top of these boards, and that was a piece of

5.10. (*Right*) Looking down on the 2012 excavation of the East Barracks. This 5 × 5 m area contains the fireplace discovered in 2011.

5.11. (*Bottom left*) Examples of the pieces of cut lead that are abundant at the north end of the East Barracks. (Similar pieces of cut lead were found inside the well.) These may have been weights to hold down the hems of garments. The scale is marked in centimeters and inches.

5.12. (*Bottom right*) Shot and musket balls found in quantity at the north end of the East Barracks. These were discovered in the charcoal that surrounds the barracks fireplace.

burned cloth (fig. 5.14). Blackened beyond recognition, it was thick with a coarse weave, and it was the only cloth to be discovered at the fort since the 1950s, when Gifford found a "charred blanket" (fig. 5.15) (1955, 59).

Unfortunately after we exposed the bottom boards and carefully removed the charred cloth, our trench experienced a major cave-in. We shored up the walls, removed what must have been a ton or more of dirt that had fallen into the trench, and continued our work. For a barracks building where we

5.13. (*Top left*) David Starbuck excavating burned boards at the bottom of the east wall of the East Barracks. A relatively small area was exposed, and much more needs to be seen to fully understand the positioning of the wood.

5.14. (*Top right*) Heavily charred cloth found in the East Barracks in 2012.

5.15. (*Left*) The remains of a charred blanket discovered by Stanley Gifford. Fort William Henry Museum.

had truly feared that all artifacts might have been removed in the 1950s, we were making major *in situ* discoveries in the lower half of the cellar. Luck was with us, and we weren't about to stop.

An important goal of future excavations should be to outline the entire surface of the East Barracks for visitors. After all, every visitor to a historic site wants to know how accurate the reconstruction is, and Fort William Henry is no exception. Because the buildings at the fort were not reconstructed precisely on their original foundations in the 1950s, archeology could be an extremely helpful tool for locating all building foundations, for marking their perimeters on the surface, and for creating new exhibits that would help visitors visualize the layout of the original fort more precisely.

Dumps outside the East Curtain Wall of the Fort

Beginning in the 1990s, we have devoted a great deal of effort to understanding the dumps that lie outside the East Curtain Wall of the reconstructed fort. (In previous seasons these were referred to simply as the dumps east of the fort, but since 2011 this area has been called "the East Curtain Wall," reflecting the adjacent, outermost log wall of the fort.) We have excavated a great many trenches and test pits across the slope east of the fort (fig. 5.16), but it was not until 2012 that it became very clear that most of the debris from the period of the fort's occupation (1755–57) lies within a layer of dark brown soil about 30 to 40 cm thick (about 16 in) that is about 1.25 to 1.60 m (4 to 5 ft) below the modern surface (fig. 5.17). There are other historic materials that lie above this, and prehistoric materials that lie both above and below, but within this band of dark soil are many thousands of butchered bone fragments and numerous British artifacts (fig. 5.18). And very importantly, there is a layer of charcoal 2 cm (1 in) thick at the surface of the dark brown layer.

What this means is that we have a layer that represents the burning of the fort, and it clearly marks the surface of a thick cultural layer that represents the years 1755–57. Within this cultural layer at one of the fort's dumps, we have thousands of butchered bones, much pottery, wine bottles, buttons and buckles, melted lead, tobacco pipes, and all of the other trash that built up within a British frontier fort (see table 5.1). There were few artifacts in the charcoal that lies on the surface, and few in the first 10 cm of the dump; artifacts (and bones) were the densest 10 to 20 cm into this layer. Between 1997–99 and 2011–12, we have excavated perhaps 10 percent of the sloping dump areas east of the fort, and many of our trenches went only to the bottom of the historic deposits. This area outside the East Curtain Wall thus retains a lot of potential for future research, especially if the objective is to reach the deeper, Native American occupations.

As mentioned in chapter 2, the dumps are relatively deep because soil (and artifacts) from the parade ground were pushed down this slope, creating reverse stratigraphy close to the surface. It is quite surprising to find prehistoric artifacts both above and below the main layer from the time of the fort's occupation. The only *in situ* features on this slope are the two Native American roasting platforms; everything else appears to be the result of simple dumping from higher up the slope. There is nothing here to suggest dumping from a particular building that once stood in the parade

5.16. Excavating outside the East Curtain Wall of the fort in 2012, facing northeast. The small canopies are a reminder of how hot the sun can be against the side of the fort.

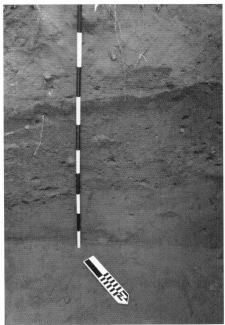

5.17. (*Left*) The thick, dark soil layer in this pit is the main occupation zone of the fort—all artifacts in this layer within the dump date from between 1755 and 1757. The light brown layer below it contains only prehistoric materials, and the mottled layer above it contains a bulldozed mixture of artifacts from all time periods. The arrow points north, and the vertical rod is marked in 10-cm units.

5.18. (*Above right*) Chelsey Cook, a student from Plymouth State University, holds a piece of grapeshot that she just found outside the East Curtain Wall.

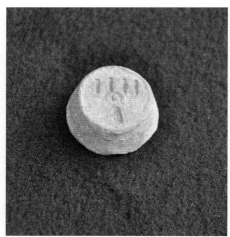

5.19. (*Left*) Sherds from a single mug of Nottingham stoneware with bread crumb decoration. This most definitely was not regular issue at the fort. Was it a favorite personal mug brought to the fort by an officer?

5.20. (*Right*) A lead weight or stamp (111.9 grams) found outside the East Curtain Wall. It measures 3.2 cm (1.26 in) in diameter at the base and 2.7 cm (1.06 in) in diameter at the top, and it is 1.7 cm (0.67 in) high.

ground, and nothing to suggest that the trash came from officers as opposed to enlisted men.

Food remains predominate here, and most butchered bones are from large mammals such as cows and pigs (see appendix 2). No plant remains were observed, and no soil flotation has been conducted here for the retrieval of small ecofacts, such as seeds, nutshells, and animal bones (although soil samples were saved for this purpose). Artifacts recovered in 2011–12 were similar to those found in 1997–99, including gunflints; musket balls; two British farthings, both dated to 1749; grapeshot; wine bottles; and sherds of delftware, buff-bodied and slip-decorated earthenware, and white salt-glazed stoneware. Distinctive new discoveries included sherds of lustrous Nottingham stoneware (circa 1700–1810), which we had never found before (fig. 5.19), and a lead weight (fig. 5.20). However, not every find in the dump was equally significant. In 2011 our discoveries outside the East Curtain Wall included a cat skeleton in a bag, a plastic mermaid, and a live skunk (which had to be helped out of the trench it had fallen into).

The Significance of the Latest Archeology

The recent return of archeology to Fort William Henry has had many positive aspects because archeologists have become more of a catalyst for change in the fort's exhibits and in its overall presentation to the public. Most of the board members of the French and Indian War Society — based at the fort — have been members of our archeological team, and we all share an interest in what happens next.

Until now, most Americans have had what might be termed a "*Last of the Mohicans* perspective" on this fort and on the French and Indian War in general. Unquestionably we are all heavily influenced by the fiction of James Fenimore Cooper. But now, thanks to archeology, we hope that the results of our new generation of research will better inform visitors about the artifacts and features that have actually survived from the 1750s. We will increasingly see Fort William Henry through the eyes of the archeologist as new exhibits are opened.

When viewed in that light, the research conducted in 2011–12 has demonstrated that even structures that saw heavy disturbance by power equipment in the 1950s still have the potential to contain significant features and artifacts. Historical photographs taken in the 1950s show massive soil removal from the East Barracks, yet we found the base of a fireplace, spent ammunition that suggested the final destruction of the building by the French, and numerous artifacts that included a nearly unique brass arrowhead and burned cloth. It is never too late to learn more from a disturbed building site, and our discovery that much of the 1750s dumping outside the fort was within a single, concentrated soil layer enabled us to focus on that layer for most of the 2012 season. Because of extensive regrading of the landscape, four prior field seasons (1997–99 and 2011) had not revealed to us that the fort's main dump was within such a discrete, concentrated zone. There had been so much "noise" from stratigraphic disturbances that we had utterly failed to see how clear and distinct the main occupation zone really is. It is definitely quite satisfying when new research succeeds in making such significant discoveries.

The Dead Have Stories to Tell

Forensic Anthropology at the Fort

ON MARCH 29, 2012, the National Geographic Channel aired a program titled "The Last Mohican?" in its cold-case forensics series, *The Decrypters*. New research conducted on one of the human skeletons discovered at Fort William Henry, identified as "Burial 14," had just revealed the DNA of a Native American who had been buried in the British cemetery outside the fort. For a Native American to be buried side by side with his British allies was most likely a fairly rare occurrence, but even more significantly this was a Native American who had grown up in the American West, two thousand miles from his final resting place. Such a possibility — a tremendous journey from west to east in the mid-eighteenth century — had never occurred to researchers before, and this amazing discovery was but the latest finding to be made through the analysis of skeletons unearthed at the fort in the 1950s and the 1990s.

In this case and many others, credit goes to the exciting field of forensic anthropology, identified as a distinct field only since the 1970s. Forensic anthropology has proved extremely successful in analyzing human bones to determine age, sex, race, stature, disease, pathologies, trauma, and cause of death. Early American forts such as Fort William Henry often have associated cemeteries with unmarked graves, containing individuals who died from disease, noncombatant injuries, or battle-related trauma. Forensic anthropology has helped greatly in assigning an identity to these long-forgotten soldiers. All the same, in every case it is important to remember that these human remains deserve respectful treatment, and they should be disturbed only by trained professionals who have appropriate research questions.

We do not know precisely how many soldiers and civilians died and were buried in the village of Lake George between 1755 (the Battle of Lake George) and 1775 (the beginning of the American Revolution). Nevertheless, we believe that disease, injuries, and raids may have killed 500 or more members of the British garrison of Fort William Henry between its construction in 1755 and the British surrender to the French in August 1757. As many as

6.1. The log exhibit building that was built to house ten skeletons excavated at Fort William Henry in the 1950s. The bones were removed from view in 1993, and large photographs on the walls depict the skeletons as they formerly appeared in this location.

200 or more were then killed in the massacre on August 10; and perhaps in excess of 1,000 died in Lake George in the mid-1770s, when this community was home to the most extensive smallpox hospitals in the British colonies. In summary, then, perhaps as many as 2,000 individuals died in Lake George during the mid- to late-eighteenth century, and virtually none of their graves has survived down to the present day with a marker of any sort (fig. 6.1).

Skeletons First Exposed in the 1950s

The largest concentration of human remains at Fort William Henry is in the unmarked cemetery that lies about 200 feet southwest of the reconstructed fort. It was in the mid-1950s that Stanley Gifford deliberately sought and then exposed ten skeletons at one corner of this cemetery (figs. 6.2, 6.3); he also encountered scattered skeletal remains, sometimes incomplete, throughout the charred ruins of the fort (fig. 6.4). Newspaper reports at the time indicated that "the graveyard was discovered after topsoil was cleared by a bulldozer. When the undisturbed sub-soil was reached, grave lines could be discerned by variations of color in the soil" (McGary 1953). Although no detailed forensic analysis survives from the time of Gifford's work, contemporary newspaper accounts trace his progress in the winter of 1953–54 and describe the heating cables and blankets provided by General Electric that enabled him to continue working in the military cemetery during cold weather. Thermostats made sure that the temperature in the

6.2. The excavation inside the military cemetery in 1954. The sides of the log exhibit building have already been constructed, and the raised pedestals represent skeletons waiting to be excavated. Fort William Henry Museum.

6.3. A promotional picture from the 1950s. An interpreter is posing with the skeletons in the military cemetery. Fort William Henry Museum.

open graves was a constant 40 degrees. As Gifford exposed the skeletons in the cemetery, he observed that one had a musket ball in its elbow, another had its feet tied together, and a third had a flattened musket ball resting next to a vertebra (fig. 6.5).

In addition to remains uncovered in the formal cemetery, the skeletons of five soldiers were exposed in 1957 underneath a brick floor at the south end of the East Barracks (figs. 6.6, 6.7). Their bodies had been hastily buried, possibly under the floor of a hospital room in the barracks, and their bones were quite disjointed and scattered when found. Carleton Dunn was called in to identify the bones at that time (Dunn, personal communication, July

6.4. (*Right*) A human skeleton discovered in the ruins of the fort in the 1950s. Fort William Henry Museum.

6.5. (*Below*) A plan view of skeletons in the military cemetery, July 29, 1954. Seven skeletons had been exposed thus far, and three more (labeled as "MOLD") were still awaiting excavation. Artifacts found with the skeletons are identified on the drawing. Fort William Henry Museum.

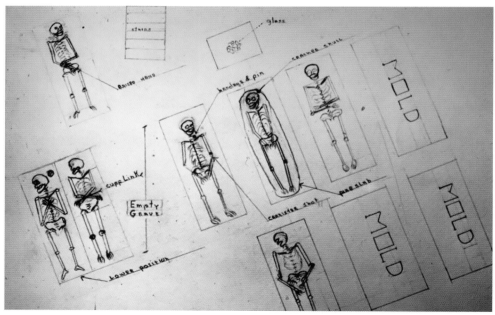

6.6. Stanley Gifford excavating skeletons at the south end of the East Barracks in 1957, the area now known as "The Crypt." Fort William Henry Museum.

6.7. The skeletons in The Crypt after further excavation. Fort William Henry Museum.

19, 2012). Their remains showed signs of scalping and mutilation, and one of the skeletons had eight musket balls lodged in its bones. Another skeleton was even missing its skull, and this last soldier had been deliberately beheaded — his second cervical (neck) vertebra had been cut clean through.

We know from history that Fort William Henry surrendered to the French on August 9, 1757, and soon after — as the garrison was leaving the fort — some of the Native Americans attached to the French army raced inside the fort and killed and scalped about seventeen sick and wounded British soldiers. Are these five skeletons the remains of some of the soldiers who came to that tragic end?

6.8. The five skeletons in The Crypt at the conclusion of the excavation. Fort William Henry Museum.

Father Pierre Roubaud was a French Jesuit priest who accompanied General Montcalm's army, and in his journal he described a warrior who "carried in his hand a human head, from which trickled streams of blood, and which he displayed as the most splendid prize he could have secured" (quoted in Steele 1990, 111).

Gifford may very well have discovered the very soldier whose head was described by Father Roubaud. To make matters worse, on the next day—August 10—the rest of the British army was attacked by Indians on the Military Road that ran south to Fort Edward. Thus the murder of the five soldiers in this very spot in the fort may be viewed as the unfortunate prelude to the ensuing massacre on the road to Fort Edward, the exact location of which has never been determined.

The five skeletons found in the East Barracks were subsequently laid out very neatly in an exhibit titled "The Crypt," and they remained on display through 1993, at which time they were removed to be studied by forensic anthropologists (fig. 6.8). Out of respect for these fallen soldiers, no bones are currently on display in this exhibit (fig. 6.9) (see appendix 1).

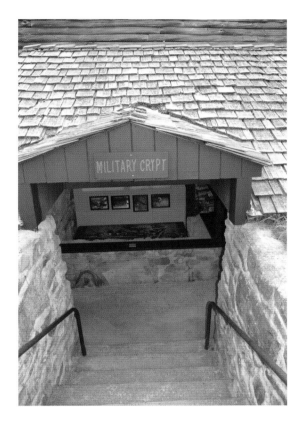

6.9. The Military Crypt as it appears today, with new exhibits inside.

New Research in the 1990s

In 1993 Maria Liston, then a professor at Adirondack Community College, was asked if she would be able to study the fort's skeletons prior to reburial. She was soon joined by Dr. Brenda Baker of the New York State Museum, and — assisted by students and volunteers — they jointly reanalyzed many of the remains that had been found in the 1950s (figs. 6.10, 6.11). The bones in "The Crypt" were especially revealing:

> All of the individuals buried in the crypt display evidence of longstanding infection in their skeletons, including both active and healed lesions. In four of the five skeletons, there is evidence of unhealed pre-mortem trauma. . . . three of the skeletons have perimortem trauma consistent with musket ball wounds. A fragment of metal, possibly a knife blade, was found on the legs of the individual designated Crypt 5. There is also evidence of other perimortem trauma on all of the skeletons, including blows and cuts on the head, and to the chest and abdomen, consistent with eyewitness accounts of the massacre and its aftermath. (Liston and Baker 1995, 29)

6.10. Maria Liston (left) and Brenda Baker studying a skeleton in the military cemetery in 1993. The dark appearance of the bones is due to alvar, a liquid plastic preservative that had coated the bones since the 1950s. Dirt had stuck to the bones over the intervening years, and Liston and Baker needed to remove the preservative so they could proceed with their analysis.

Although injuries such as these appear consistent with an attack on the sick and injured who had remained behind in the fort, there also was much evidence that the bodies had been mutilated:

> The pattern of the cuts and slashes suggests strongly that these men were mutilated possibly to obtain trophies. . . . The head was taken from one man; scalps may have been taken from the others. . . . In all the men, ribs were cut or fractured at the sternal ends or sides, probably to obtain access to the chest cavity so the heart could be reached. The fact that the pubic area is cut in all of the men suggests genital mutilation. The extent of destruction in the abdominal and chest cavities indicates the men may also have been disemboweled. (Liston and Baker 1995, 41)

This work was featured in the program "The Last of the Mohicans" in the series *Archaeology* on The Learning Channel that first aired in the fall of 1993.

Liston and Baker returned to the cemetery in 1995 and located an additional six skeletons, three of which were exhumed and featured on *The New Detectives* on the Discovery Channel in 1995. Two of the three were tentatively identified in a news report at the time as being "one black, the other of mixed race" (Blackwell 1996). The report also noted that "small fragments of woolen cloth found in the graves yielded fossilized fly eggs. Since the graves were three feet under — too deep for flies to get in — Baker concluded the bodies were probably buried after they'd already begun to decompose" (ibid.).

Throughout the 1990s research, the skeletons at Fort William Henry proved to be extremely rich in information about some of the injuries and diseases that affected soldiers at the time of the French and Indian War. For example, many soldiers had herniated disks from carrying loads that were much too heavy, and their bones also revealed evidence of arthritis, infections, and abscessed teeth. Liston and Baker discovered evidence of several types of trauma, including decapitations, cut marks in the chest and stomach areas, and indications that a number of men had been shot, especially in the knee. Clearly the bones of the soldiers demonstrate that life at this frontier outpost could be dangerous and deadly, and they also suggest that punishing physical labor was commonplace at the fort.

6.11. Brenda Baker and a student, Janet Truelove, reassembling a skull from the military cemetery.

Burial 14: New Perspectives

In March 2011 I was contacted by Glenn Swift, an assistant producer with the British television series *History Cold Case*, and he asked whether we might have a skeleton at the fort that would be a suitable subject for an American version of the series, to be titled *The Decrypters*, which would appear on the National Geographic Channel. Swift was looking for cold cases in the United States, skeletons already in collections that could tell new stories when subjected to the latest forensic testing. Several eighteenth- and nineteenth-century cases were being chosen from across the United States, and the producer was eager to include one of the individuals from the cemetery at Fort William Henry as they conducted DNA testing and facial recon-struction. I suggested one skeleton — since named "Burial 14"— because of the 1990s claim that it might be the remains of an African American. After all, his skull had features that were definitely not Caucasian. The remains had been placed in between British soldiers, buried in rows, who had prob-ably died of disease months prior to the siege and massacre. (It is unlikely that any burials were made outside the fort walls after the siege began.) Con-sequently there was little chance of this having been an individual aligned with the French army during the final destruction of the fort.

After the fort's skeletons were removed from display, Baker transported most of the more intact skeletons to Arizona State University, when she took a position there, and made that skeleton available to Dr. Michelle Hamilton and other researchers at the Forensic Anthropology Center at Texas State University–San Marcos, as they sought to determine the race and origin of this distinctive-looking individual. Hamilton and her forensics team con-ducted the analysis, which included a computed tomography (CT) scan, DNA testing, and carbon and nitrogen isotope analysis, and quickly de-termined that this person had been a Native American, so it was initially assumed that he must have grown up locally (hence the program was titled "The Last Mohican?"). However, it was not until his dental enamel was stud-ied that it became clear he had lived in the Western United States while growing up, probably in the Dakotas, Wyoming, Utah, or Idaho. Isotope testing demonstrated that while his teeth were being formed (before the age of fifteen), the water he consumed existed only in the West.

This raises provocative questions. By any remote chance could he have been a Native American who traveled to Lake George with French forces? The Texas-based researchers do not believe so, because traces of insect remains (fly casings) suggest that his body had lain out in the open for quite some time before being committed to the grave. Besides, if he had accompanied the French army, there would have been signs of trauma on the bones (the result of having been killed in the siege), but the only marks on his bones were healed fractures in his right cheek and arm (Carola 2012) and broken nasal bones. He had most likely died, the researchers believe, of a fast-moving disease such as smallpox (although other diseases are a possibility).

But how had he survived a two-thousand-mile journey, crossing the United States nearly fifty years before Meriwether Lewis and William Clark made their famous journey from east to west? And had he become a British scout, serving and dying with his new allies prior to the final French at-tack? Native Americans most definitely served with the British army during the French and Indian War, but they were typically Stockbridge Mohicans and Mohawks (Iroquois), not visitors from far away. We clearly need more information about the movements of Native Americans in the eighteenth

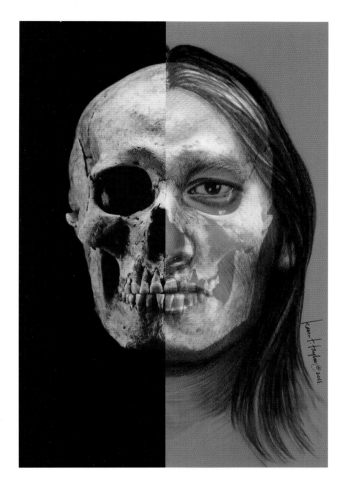

6.12. The face of Burial 14, one of the brave defenders of Fort William Henry. This skull-based reconstruction puts a very human face on skeletal remains from the military cemetery. © Karen T. Taylor; used with permission of the artist.

century, but this is powerful evidence that these people may have traveled far greater distances in the early historic period than we ever imagined.

Using the skull from Burial 14, hand-drawn studies were created by Karen T. Taylor, a long-time forensic artist with a background in law enforcement. Based on the frontal and profile 2D reconstructions done by Taylor, digital animator Tony Reynolds created 3D digital images (fig. 6.12). It is a strong, mature man's face with high cheekbones that suggests considerable inner strength. He was between twenty-five and forty years of age, and as a defender of the fort together with British and colonial forces, he deserves to be honored and respected by modern audiences. Above all, he helps change attitudes toward the role of Native Americans at Fort William Henry. Generations have viewed them as the destroyers of the fort, as those who dug up the cemetery and committed the massacre, but we now have a powerful Native American defender of the fort whose story deserves to be told with pride and admiration.

How Do We Honor the Fort's Dead?

The skeletons discovered throughout the ruins of Fort William Henry have been taken off display so as not to disrespect the memory of these early American heroes, and many have been subjected to detailed forensic analysis. But what now? Must all of these individuals be reinterred, or is it appropriate for any of them to be kept in secure facilities where new forensic techniques may be used in the future to provide additional information about them? Decisions are still being made, and it is critical to adhere to the Native American Graves Protection and Repatriation Act (NAGPRA) of 1990, even though it may be extremely difficult to establish which nation today is most closely affiliated with Burial 14.

Perhaps the one principle that all can agree on is that each of these warriors who died in Lake George was buried by his friends with the expectation that burial would be permanent. Therefore every skeleton should be returned as closely as possible to its original resting place, whether or not that is above or below ground. Modern science needs to be respectful of the wishes of these men's communities, whether Native American or European American, but there needs to be a measure of flexibility so that the deceased individuals can teach us meaningful and positive information about their lives and cultures.

Artifacts Discovered at the Fort

7

EVERY SUMMER THAT WE DIG at Fort William Henry, we have operated a field laboratory somewhere on the grounds of the fort, either within a reconstructed barracks building or inside the Cemetery Building that is south of the fort's parking lot (fig. 7.1). A visit to our field lab in the 1990s found Merle Parsons, a retired school teacher, in charge, and her successor in 2011 and 2012 was Elizabeth "Betty" Hall, yet another retired school teacher with a passion for archeology. Thousands of visitors have now had a chance to visit our summer labs at the fort, where they can watch volunteers wash, sort, and identify artifacts. A great many of these visitors have stayed to ask questions, which is fine with us because we like to believe that our work is meaningful and pleasurable for others. After all, why spend hundreds of hours washing pottery sherds and rusty nails if they aren't going to provide interesting stories for visitors?

Our processing and identification of artifacts has continued every winter at Plymouth State University, where literally thousands of fragments of glass, pottery, nails, bones, and armaments have been cleaned, bagged, and entered into artifact catalogs on a computer. The old adage that laboratory work takes at least three times as long as actual excavation is, if anything, an underestimate. As ongoing analyses are completed, artifacts from recent excavations are gradually being added to those from the 1950s excavations and kept in secure storage rooms at Fort William Henry. Although many of the best artifacts discovered during the 1950s are currently on display, there are many others that have always been in storage or that periodically rotate between storage and display as exhibits are updated. Over a hundred boxes of artifacts recovered between 1997 and the present are now in the process of being added to the fort's permanent collections, thanks to the field work of the State University of New York Adirondack archeologists, the laboratory work at Plymouth State University, and especially the identifications of Betty Hall.

A rich body of literature describing eighteenth-century artifacts has been created by archeologists and specialists in early American material culture. Preeminent among these are *A Guide to Artifacts of Colonial America* (Noel Hume 1969) and *Fort Michilimackinac 1715–1781* (Stone 1974), but other excellent artifact descriptions are also available in Michael Coe (2006), and Lynn

7.1. Identifying artifacts inside the cemetery building in the summer of 2012.

Evans (2003), Jacob Grimm (1970), Lee Hanson and Dick Ping Hsu (1975), Karlis Karklins (2000), George Neumann and Frank Kravic (1975), Catherine Sullivan (1986), and David Starbuck (2010). In addition, every archeological site report typically includes lists of the artifacts found, permitting detailed comparisons from site to site. These comparisons are essential in order to investigate sources of supply, the routes along which supplies traveled, and consumer choices (personal preferences) in the eighteenth century.

At an even deeper level, analysis of the artifacts recovered through archeology permits interpretations about the quality of life when people were far from their original homes and the degree to which the latest innovations in consumer goods had spread to frontier settings. Thus at Fort William Henry we need to ask whether the armaments, tools, tableware, provisions, and personal artifacts were the same as at contemporary British forts and domestic sites in the colonies. And if not, why not? Because this was an outpost on the far frontier of colonial America, should we assume that soldiers possessed "just the basics"? Were there any amenities, any traces of the lives that soldiers and officers had known back home in England or in the American colonies?

The 1950s

When the northwest bastion of Fort William Henry was excavated in the 1950s, Stanley Gifford and his team uncovered a superlative collection of armaments that included large quantities of musket balls, smaller lead shot,

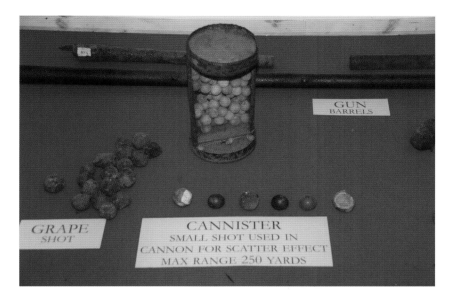

GUN
BARRELS

GRAPE
SHOT

CANNISTER
SMALL SHOT USED IN
CANNON FOR SCATTER EFFECT
MAX RANGE 250 YARDS

7.2. Grapeshot and canister shot from the 1950s excavation, on display in the West Barracks.

grapeshot, and canister shot (fig. 7.2), bayonets, halberds, fragments of mortar shells, and gunflints — that is, a very military assemblage. (Examples of these are illustrated in Starbuck 2010.) This was superb evidence of the French assault on the fort and the British defense of it. In the parade ground and barracks areas, Gifford also discovered a more domestic assemblage, including pottery and glass, hoes, spades, tobacco pipes, buttons, and all of the paraphernalia of daily life. A very significant find by Gifford was "one button of the Second Battalion of the Pennsylvania Line" (1955, 54), evidence of an American presence at the site during the American Revolution, twenty years after the fort's destruction. Records have not survived that describe exactly where most of these objects were found, but the extensive 1950s collections provide strong evidence that nearly two hundred years of occasional collecting and digging in the ruins of the fort had not seriously compromised the integrity of the site. An amazing amount of material has survived up until the present day.

The storage areas that contain Gifford's finds hold thousands of wrought iron nails, spikes, tobacco pipes, wine bottle fragments, musket balls, and buckshot; as well as hundreds of gunflints, mortar shell fragments, and plain metal buttons; dozens of ax heads, knives, bayonet fragments, and buckles; and lesser numbers of tin canteen fragments and pewter spoon fragments. There also are chunks of charcoalized beams in the storage collection, reflecting the nearly intact timbers that were often found while digging the East Barracks. Curiously, the collection includes very few butchered animal bones, making it difficult to say much about the soldiers' diet, and there are very few pottery sherds from the period. Most likely some categories of artifacts and ecofacts simply were not saved, and this reflects the shifting priorities of archeologists from the 1950s to the present. We modern-day archeologists profess that we save everything, but no doubt archeologists of the future will claim that, like our predecessors, we did not save enough.

1997 to the Present

Many of the artifacts recovered during excavations between 1997 and 2000 have already been published (Starbuck 2002 and 2010), but all artifacts recovered between 1997 and the present were reexamined in the fall of 2012. At that time every diagnostic artifact was studied, looking for distinctive patterns that would make life at the fort more real and that would tell new stories about what it was like to live under the constant threat of attack. I have personally examined all of this material, sorting out the gunflints, musket balls, grapeshot, canister shot, fragments of mortar shells, buttons, buckles, cuff links, coins, and a very substantial quantity of prehistoric material.

On the whole these artifacts are somewhat more fragmentary than those recovered in the 1950s. It appears that many of our excavation areas had been systematically combed for large artifacts some sixty years ago, because everything that we find today is quite small or fragmentary when compared to the older collections at the fort. With modern excavations, all dirt is sifted through hardware cloth with a quarter-inch mesh. When smaller artifacts such as beads are observed, we switch to an eighth-inch mesh or even to tea strainers. Even the smallest artifacts may tell a story, although they might not look as impressive as larger ones in a display case.

Following are descriptions of a selection of key artifacts uncovered at Fort William Henry between 1997 and the present.

BUCKLES

Fragments of twenty-four dress buckles of brass were discovered at the fort in the 1990s, and another four buckle fragments were found in 2011–12. The majority of these were discovered either in the West Barracks or in the dump outside the East Curtain Wall (most are depicted in fig. 7.3). Every one of these is quite fragmentary, and clearly they were not discarded until their usefulness was gone.

BUTTONS

Buttons are typically one of the most personal artifacts that archeologists can hope to find, and the archeologist is often able to feel a very close connection with the soldier or officer who seemingly lost a button. Numbered

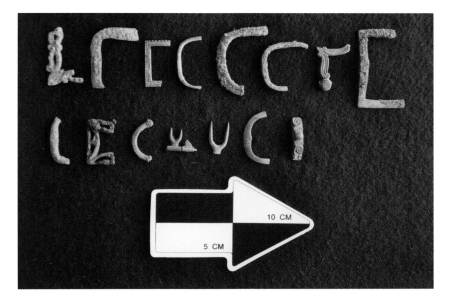

7.3. Fragments of brass buckles. All buckle fragments in the top row are from the dump east of the fort. In the bottom row, the five buckle fragments and tines on the left are from the West Barracks, and the two buckle fragments on the right are from the north end of the parade ground.

regimental buttons did not appear until years after the French and Indian War was over, so the buttons found at Fort William Henry are largely undecorated and rather plain in appearance. Very large numbers of these were found at the fort in the 1950s, and many of these are on display today in the reconstructed West Barracks.

In the 1990s we discovered eighty-eight metal buttons (brass and pewter), three wood buttons, and one bone button. The vast majority of these were recovered from the West Barracks foundation, from the north end of the parade ground, and from the dump outside the East Curtain Wall. Many of the buttons found in the remains of the West Barracks are pictured in fig. 7.4, and those from the parade ground appear in fig. 7.5. During the 2011–12 excavations, we found an additional seven metal buttons in the East Barracks, and one metal button and one bone button were discovered in the outside dump.

The presence of a small quantity of numbered regimental buttons is a definite indication that soldiers either camped or visited here during the American Revolution, twenty years after the fort was destroyed. We found one 2nd Battalion Pennsylvania button at the north end of the parade ground; and there was a 1st Battalion Pennsylvania and an American 22nd Regiment button in the foundation of the West Barracks. (Both of the West Barracks buttons are pictured in fig. 7.6.) The site of Fort William Henry has attracted visitors ever since the massacre of 1757, and perhaps these buttons were left by some of the earliest tourists at the site.

7.4. The obverses of brass and pewter buttons found in the West Barracks, along with one two-holed wood button (*top row, center*).

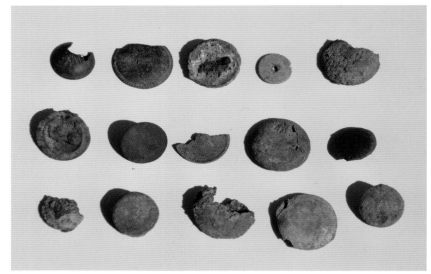

7.5. The obverses of brass and pewter buttons found at the north end of the parade ground, along with one one-holed bone button (*top row, second from right*).

7.6. Continental Army brass buttons, both found in the West Barracks. The button on the left is from the American 22nd Regiment, and the button on the right is from the 1st Battalion Pennsylvania.

7.7. Sets of brass cuff-links. *Top row, left to right:* These were found in the West Barracks, the West Barracks, and the north end of the parade ground. *Bottom row, left to right:* These were found at the south end of the parade ground, at the south end of the parade ground, and in the dump outside the East Curtain Wall.

CUFF LINKS

Eight sets of brass cuff links were discovered by our team in the 1990s, scattered among the parade ground, the West Barracks, and the dump outside the East Curtain Wall (most of these are depicted in fig. 7.7). One additional brass cuff link was found in the dump in 2012. Since these were worn by officers, they are among the truest status indicators to have been found in the fort.

CLOTHING FASTENERS (HOOKS AND EYES)

Hooks and eyes are extremely rare in the site, and just three eyes were found during our excavations (fig. 7.8). Of the various French and Indian War sites that have been excavated in Lake George and Fort Edward, only the house of a sutler (a civilian merchant) in Fort Edward (Starbuck 2010) has been found to contain a significant number of clothing fasteners (ninety-four altogether).

FABRIC

The survival of fabric or leather in archeological sites is rare, but charring definitely increases either material's chances of survival. Since Fort William Henry burned in its entirety, that would seem to improve the likelihood of finding charred cloth. Gifford (1955, 59) found what appeared to be a burned blanket in the 1950s (fig. 5.15), and our team found what appears to be a small quantity of burned linen at the base of the east wall of the East Barracks in 2012 (fig. 5.14).

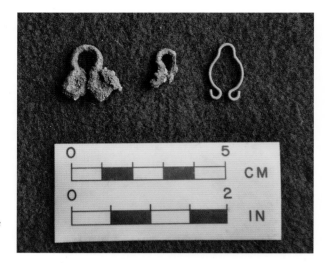

7.8. Iron and brass clothing fasteners (eyes). These were found (from left to right) at the south end of the parade ground, in the dump outside the East Curtain Wall, and in the West Barracks.

BEADS

We recovered only one bead of shell at Fort William Henry (fig. 2.10) and virtually no beads of glass (which might have been expected if people at this outpost traded with Native Americans). However, this fort was clearly not intended to serve as a trading post, so the shell bead is an anomaly. It may have belonged to any of the protagonists here, or even to a Native American from a much earlier period.

RING

One undecorated brass ring was found inside the West Barracks (see Starbuck 2002, fig. 5.16). Although it is quite unremarkable in appearance, its presence is unusual: only a very few rings have been found at other French and Indian War sites in the area.

JEW'S HARPS (MOUTH HARPS)

This simple musical instrument is represented by just two examples — both made of iron — that were found in the dump outside the East Curtain Wall (Starbuck 2002, fig. 5.20; Starbuck 2010, fig. 9.3). Such low numbers are typical of each of the sites in the Lake George and Fort Edward area, and there is no archeological evidence at Fort William Henry of any other type of musical instrument.

TOBACCO PIPES

If tobacco pipes are a good indicator of leisure time, then the soldiers and officers at Fort William Henry did have at least one favorite vice. All of the British military sites in the Lake George and Fort Edward area have revealed

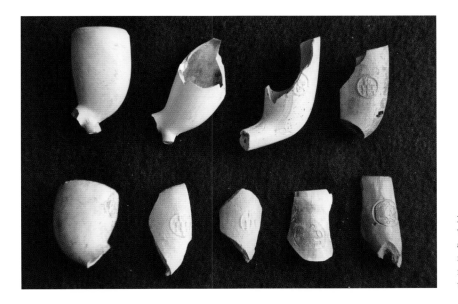

7.9. Tobacco pipe bowls with Robert Tippet's and William Mamby's maker's marks, from many different areas on the fort grounds.

sizable numbers of white, mold-made tobacco pipes, even allowing for the fact that every long pipestem breaks into at least a half-dozen fragments. Clearly tobacco was available in quantity, and sutlers would have been all too eager to provide both tobacco and pipes to British soldiers. We are not aware of whether sutlers based at Fort William Henry had pipes to sell, but they would have been available in quantity at the nearby sutlers' houses in Fort Edward (Starbuck 2010).

A great many tobacco pipes were discovered during the 1950s excavations, and many of these are on display on the first floor of the reconstructed West Barracks, while others are in storage in collection rooms at the fort. Our excavations at the fort in the 1990s recovered 1,071 pipestem fragments, with bore diameters of either $\frac{4}{64}$ or $\frac{5}{64}$ of an inch (appropriate to the second half of the eighteenth century), and most of these were found in the outside dump or in the foundation of the West Barracks. More recently, we found another 49 stem fragments and 16 bowl fragments in the East Barracks, and 81 stem fragments in the dump outside the East Curtain Wall. A great many of the pipe bowls have the maker's mark (and sometimes the cartouche) of their manufacturer, in this case either Robert Tippet ("RT") of Bristol, England, or William Mamby ("WM") of London, England. Examples of pipe bowls with maker's marks appear in figure 7.9.

NEEDLES, SCISSORS, PINS, AND THIMBLES

Sewing supplies are most common in the West Barracks, and in that foundation we found a brass thimble, a sewing needle, eighteen straight pins, and a pair of scissors (some of these are pictured in fig. 7.10). We also found

7.10. Sewing supplies. The brass thimble, the needle (*top row, left*) and the bottom row of pins are all from the West Barracks. The rest of the pins were found throughout the fort grounds.

two pins at the north end and one at the south end of the parade ground, three near the cemetery area, and two in the dump outside the East Curtain Wall. These are modest numbers, to be sure, but it must be cautioned that needles drop through sifting screens very easily, and there may originally have been many, many more. Still, when combined with related artifact types such as buttons and buckles, they are part of the growing evidence that the West Barracks is the most domestic site we have examined at Fort William Henry, with the broadest range of everyday activities that have little to do with defending or fighting at the fort.

POTTERY AND PORCELAIN

White salt-glazed stoneware, porcelain, and delftware are the most common wares that were used at Fort William Henry, although modest quantities of redware, gray salt-glazed stoneware, unrefined stoneware, and buff-bodied and slip-decorated earthenware appear here as well. (The totals for sherds recovered during the 1990s excavations appear in Starbuck 2002.) A majority of the vessels in this assemblage are cups, saucers, plates, and bowls, although the unrefined stoneware items are storage vessels (jugs and crocks). A great many of the white salt-glazed sherds had "Scratch Blue" decoration, which is very common for this period. Representative examples of these types appear in figures 7.11, 7.12, 7.13, 7.14, and 7.15.

The most recent excavations at the fort in 2011 and 2012 have discovered larger numbers of buff-bodied, slip-decorated earthenware sherds than in the past (figs. 7.16 and 7.17), which is significant because this ware is of an older date and is not usually that common at military sites from the 1750s

7.11. (*Top*) Sherds of porcelain teacups and saucers. The top row are all from the West Barracks; the bottom row are from the dump outside the East Curtain Wall.

7.12. (*Middle*) Sherds of unrefined stoneware. *Top row, left to right:* from the West Barracks and from the moat. *Bottom row:* both are from the dump outside the East Curtain Wall.

7.13. (*Bottom*) Sherds of delftware from various bowls and mugs. All are from the dump outside the East Curtain Wall.

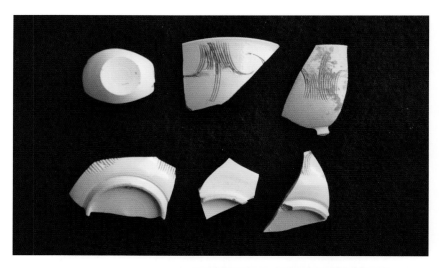

7.14. (*Above*) Sherds of white salt-glazed stoneware cups. All are from the West Barracks, and most have Scratch Blue decoration.

7.15. (*Right*) Sherds of white salt-glazed stoneware, various vessel types. All are from the dump outside the East Curtain Wall, and most have Scratch Blue decoration.

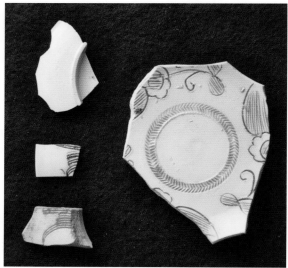

in the area. This may well be an indication of older vessels having a "lag effect" at this outpost, with some relatively "out-of-date" vessels arriving from home with some of the soldiers. Also of special interest are the sherds from a mug of Nottingham stoneware found in the dump outside the East Curtain Wall in 2012 (see fig. 5.19). This is the first example of this ware to be found at a British military site in Lake George or Fort Edward, and it must have been a truly beautiful vessel.

GLASS

Glass is present in many different forms at British military sites, sometimes consisting of fine tableware (presumably for the tables of officers), but fre-

quently as dark-green wine bottles, medicine bottles, and square-sided case bottles. An excellent literature exists on this subject by Margaret Brown (1971) and Olive Jones and E. Ann Smith (1985). It is difficult to do very much with the small quantities of window glass found at Fort William Henry—the glass was scattered widely over the years by scavengers and by the 1950s restoration, making it impossible to interpret where windows may have been located. An additional problem is that some later window glass has been mixed in, making it even more difficult to determine whether more than a very few windows were present at the original fort.

In the 1990s from throughout the fort we recovered 1,004 fragments of wine bottles, 212 fragments of case bottles, 279 fragments of tableware (wineglasses, drinking glasses, and toasting glasses), and 128 fragments of vials or medicine bottles (figs. 7.18, 7.19). Perhaps the most interesting single find was a glass seal that we uncovered at the north end of the parade ground; this would have appeared on the shoulder of a wine bottle (fig. 7.20).

These numbers were augmented in 2011 and 2012 when we discovered 129 wine bottle fragments in the East Barracks and 158 wine bottle fragments in the East Curtain Wall dump (see table 5.1). The ubiquitous wine bottle fragments to be found in every context at British military sites gives rise today to a certain amount of humor, but alcoholic beverages were no doubt much appreciated by the soldiers and officers.

FORKS, SPOONS, AND KNIVES

The dearth of eating utensils at the fort is surprising. Several hundred soldiers and officers occupied Fort William Henry for nearly two years, yet in the West Barracks we found only two fork fragments and five spoon handles, both brass and pewter (four are depicted in fig. 7.21.); and in all the sites

7.16. (*Left*) Buff-bodied, slip-decorated earthenware from the dump outside the East Curtain Wall. The scale is marked in centimeters.

7.17. (*Right*) Sherds of buff-bodied, slip-decorated earthenware. All are from the West Barracks, except for the top row, left, which is from the dump outside the East Curtain Wall.

7.18. (*Top*)
Top row: fragments
of wine glasses; left to
right: from the Military
Cemetery area, from
the West Barracks, and
from the East Barracks.
Bottom row: bases of
dark-green medicine
bottles; left to right:
from the dump out-
side the East Curtain
Wall, from the military
cemetery area, from
the West Barracks, and
from the dump outside
the East Curtain Wall.

7.19. (*Middle*)
Assorted glass vessels.
Top row, left to right:
base of a clear drinking
glass (West Barracks);
base of a clear glass bottle (dump outside the
East Curtain Wall); and
base of a clear medicine
bottle (Military Ceme-
tery area). *Bottom row,
left to right:* base of a
medicine bottle, base
of a dark-green case
bottle, and top of a
dark-green case bottle
(all from the dump out-
side the East Curtain
Wall).

7.20. (*Right*) The seal from
the shoulder of a wine bottle
found at the north end of the
parade ground in 1997.

combined we found only eight knife fragments, some with wood or bone handles (fig. 7.22). Since soldiers and officers were allowed to carry away personal possessions after the surrender, this may be yet another indication that as little as possible was left behind.

IRON HINGES

These are atypically rare at this fort. Only one hinge fragment was found in the West Barracks and one other in the dump outside the East Curtain Wall. Given the scale of these structures, there should have been many hundreds of hinges and door latches in use throughout the barracks. Their almost total absence suggests that very intense looting ("architectural salvage") must have occurred here either before or after the buildings were burned down. It raises the question of whether the French would have taken architectural hardware away with them, or whether later British armies camping in the vicinity in 1758 and 1759 would have stripped the foundations of any salvageable materials.

NAILS AND SPIKES

Hand-wrought nails and the occasional spike are among the most common — yet decidedly unglamorous — artifacts to be found at Fort William Henry. We have discovered thousands of them, especially in the West and East Barracks, and most are badly corroded. A computerized, distributional study of the nails would be useful to see if they form any type of pattern that correlates with exterior or interior walls in the barracks.

7.21. (*Left*)
Left to right: pewter spoon handle (north end of the parade ground); pewter spoon handle (dump outside the East Curtain Wall); brass spoon handle (southeast corner of the parade ground); and brass spoon bowl (West Barracks). The scale is marked in centimeters.

7.22. (*Right*)
Iron knives. All are from the dump outside the East Curtain Wall. The folding knife at the bottom has a bone handle.

FISHHOOKS

Four fishhooks have been recovered during our excavations, with one found at the south end of the parade ground, two in the West Barracks, and one in the vicinity of the military cemetery. Although this number is low, when coupled with our occasional discovery of fish bones, the presence of fishhooks does provide very direct evidence that soldiers at this outpost fished nearby, presumably in Lake George.

GUNFLINTS

Ivor Noel Hume has pointed out that "gunflints are more common on archaeological sites than are parts of the weapons themselves" (1969, 219), and that is definitely true of eighteenth-century British military sites in Lake George and Fort Edward. British and French gunflints are generally distinguishable from each other: British flints are usually gray or black and somewhat prismatic in shape, whereas French flints are honey-colored or brown and are somewhat more rounded at the back. In the 1990s we found eighty-eight French gunflints and seventy-six British gunflints at Fort William Henry, with the majority of them located at the north end of the parade ground, in the West Barracks, and in the dump east of the fort. (There also are very sizable numbers on display and in storage from the 1950s excavations.) Some of these are quite fragmentary because they were used again and again, striking the steel to touch off the spark, before finally being discarded once the flint's edge had broken completely away. We also have found occasional small flakes of flint, reflecting that breakage during use.

During our latest excavations, in 2011 and 2012, we recovered two British gunflints, eight French gunflints, and four burned gunflints from the foundation of the East Barracks; and six British gunflints, eight French gunflints, and four burned gunflints from the dump outside the East Curtain Wall. The burned gunflints are sufficiently altered in color that it is somewhat more difficult to name their country of origin. Representative gunflints from the East Barracks and the East Curtain Wall are depicted in figures 7.23, 7.24, and 7.25.

BAYONETS

Two bayonet fragments were discovered inside the foundation of the West Barracks, one of which was badly rusted but nearly complete (see Starbuck 2002, fig. 5.14). The total absence of bayonets everywhere else is surprising, given that the fort has many complete bayonets on display from the 1950s excavation.

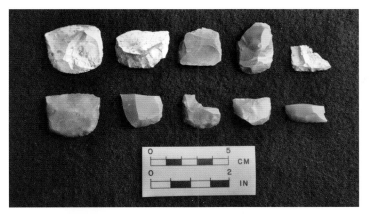

7.23. (*Top*) Gunflints found in the East Barracks. All gunflints in the top row are British, and all gunflints in the bottom row are French.

7.24. (*Middle*) Gunflints excavated in 2011 and 2012. These were found in the dump outside the East Curtain Wall. All gunflints in the top and middle rows are British, and all gunflints in the bottom row are French.

7.25. (*Bottom*) Examples of gunflints from the dump outside the East Curtain Wall, excavated between 1997 and 2000.

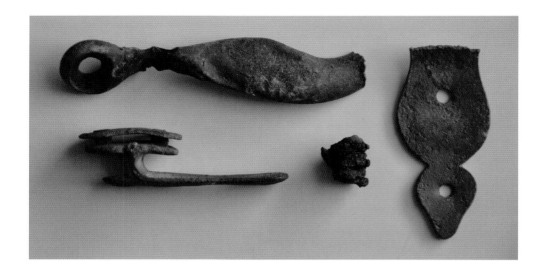

7.26. Weaponry at Fort
William Henry. *Top:*
Brown Bess side plate.
Bottom, left to right:
brass scabbard holder
(a "frog"); a worm;
and a brass escutcheon
plate. All are from the
West Barracks except
for the worm, which is
from the dump outside
the East Curtain Wall.

MUSKET PARTS

Only a very modest number of artifacts pertaining to firearms have been
recovered during recent excavations, and these consist of a single brass escutcheon plate, a brass scabbard holder (or "frog") with a bit of leather still
attached to it, a brass side plate from a Brown Bess musket, a lead gunflint
patch, and three "worms" (for extracting loads from the barrel of a musket).
The gunflint patch, which held a flint as it struck against steel, was found at
the north end of the East Barracks, and the other parts were scattered across
the fort grounds. Most of these are pictured in fig. 7.26.

MUSKET BALLS AND LEAD SHOT

Not surprisingly, musket balls are practically ubiquitous at Fort William
Henry. In the 1990s we recovered 259 musket balls and fourteen smaller
pieces of lead shot, and most of these were found in the West Barracks and
the dump outside the East Curtain Wall. These were accompanied by the
occasional bits of lead slag—the waste left over from the casting of musket
balls. Although the musket balls ranged from .57 to .69 caliber, the vast majority were between .66 and .69 caliber, which is appropriate to the British
"Brown Bess" musket.

The latest excavations at the fort recovered another twenty-three musket
balls and six pieces of lead shot in the East Barracks, and twenty musket
balls and nineteen pieces of lead shot in the dump outside the East Curtain
Wall. Some of these had been flattened on impact, and others had been
"chewed" (see fig. 7.27). Curiously, one of the musket balls from the dump
had been cut down into one-quarter of its original shape.

7.27. "Chewed" musket balls. All are from the East Barracks and were excavated in 2011 and 2012.

GRAPESHOT AND CANISTER SHOT

The 1990s excavations at the fort uncovered thirteen pieces of grapeshot and eighteen pieces of canister shot. Most of these were found at the north end (and the northwest corner) of the parade ground, where the impact of the French artillery would have been most devastating. These balls, cast of iron, are not always clearly distinguishable from each other, but in general the grapeshot is larger and perfectly round, whereas the canister shot tends to be smaller and has been shaped to fit into a canister for firing from a cannon (see fig. 7.2). The excavations at the fort in 2011 and 2012 found another seven pieces of grapeshot in the East Barracks and four pieces of grapeshot and three pieces of canister shot in the dump outside the East Curtain Wall (see figs. 7.28 and 7.29, bottom row). These balls are heavy and clearly would have been lethal when used as an antipersonnel weapon.

MORTAR SHELLS

In a very real sense, mortars brought about the destruction of Fort William Henry, as French mortar shells rained down on the fort and exploded, casting their pieces in all directions. In contrast, British mortars exploded from fatigue and were rendered useless. Eighteen fragments of mortar shells were discovered during the 1990s excavations, chiefly from where the bombardment had been the worst — the north end of the parade ground, the northwest corner of the parade ground, and the West Barracks.

7.28. Examples of grapeshot. All are from the East Barracks and were excavated in 2012.

7.29. Top row: fragments of mortar shells. Bottom row: canister shot and grapeshot. All are from the dump outside the East Curtain Wall, and all were excavated in 2012.

The excavations at the fort in 2011 and 2012 recovered eight fragments of mortar shells from the East Barracks and four pieces from the dump outside the East Curtain Wall. Two of these heavy, cast-iron chunks are pictured in figure 7.29, top row.

CUT LEAD

In 1997 several small, cut pieces of lead were discovered inside the well and at the north end of the parade ground; each measures about 1.02 × 0.75 × 0.75 cm (0.40 × 0.295 × 0.295 in). At that time, they were identified as "cut lead shot" for lack of a better designation. In 2011 and 2012 fifty-three of these small, rectangular pieces were found inside the north end of the East Barracks foundation (see fig. 5.11). These have been cut to shape, but their function is still unclear. The working hypothesis at the present time is that they may have been used as weights to hold down the hems of garments so they would hang straight.

METAL PROJECTILE POINT

As noted in chapter 5, a single brass arrowhead was discovered at the north end of the East Barracks in 2011 (fig. 5.1), and additional examples were recovered by Gifford during the 1950s. It is tempting to speculate whether Native Americans on either side used such points during the siege of 1757, but they were not found in a context that would permit that sort of dating.

AXES

Numerous ax heads were discovered in the ruins of the fort in the 1950s, but only two were recovered during our more recent work. One of these was the head of a felling ax recovered from the north end of the East Barracks in 1997, and the second was found inside the well in the same year. Several of those found in the 1950s are currently on display on the first floor of the West Barracks, including examples of belt axes.

GRINDING STONE

Part of a grinding stone was found inside the West Barracks foundation (fig. 4.14), but our excavations did not recover any other evidence for the sharpening of axes or other edged weapons.

OX SHOE

A single ox shoe was found at the northern end of the East Barracks. Given the total absence of other shoes for oxen or horses throughout the fort and its dump, this may imply that the shoe had been carried there for hammering in a blacksmith shop.

COINS

Six British halfpennies were found during the 1990s, but because of corrosion only one of these had a readable date (1730). This one was located at the north end of the parade ground. We also found two Spanish silver one-half reals (milled coins; there were none of the cruder, stamped coins known as cob money); these were located in the West Barracks and in the dump outside the East Curtain Wall (the latter coin dated to 1735). Our more recent work also found a Spanish one-half real (1751) in the East Barracks and two British copper farthings (both dated 1749) in the dump outside the East Curtain Wall. The best-preserved of these coins appear in figure 7.30.

7.30. Coins excavated from throughout the fort. *Top row, left to right:* British copper: 1730 halfpenny, 1749 farthing, and another 1749 farthing; all are from the dump outside the East Curtain Wall. *Bottom row, left to right:* Spanish silver milled coins: 1751 one-half real from the East Barracks and 1735 one-half real from the dump outside the East Curtain Wall.

The low numbers of coins were not surprising, given that relatively small numbers were found on Rogers Island and in the fort in Fort Edward (Starbuck 2004). The implication is that perhaps not very much buying and selling of goods was occurring, and only at a business establishment such as the sutler's house in Fort Edward would very many coins have been needed (see Starbuck 2010, chapter 8).

FOOD REMAINS

Almost no butchered animal bones were saved from Gifford's excavations in the 1950s, but this was definitely not because the soldiers were vegetarians. We have recovered nearly 40,000 bone fragments so far, chiefly from the dump outside the East Curtain Wall, and that represents the excavation of perhaps 5–10 percent of just one dump (fig. 7.31). The garrison at Fort William Henry had fresh meat, and seemingly substantial quantities of it. That was not always the case at military outposts: Fort Ligonier, near Pittsburgh, Pennsylvania, is a classic example of an outpost that received almost all of its meat salted, and relatively few bones have been found at that site (Guilday 1970). At Fort William Henry we have found chiefly bones of cows and pigs, with considerably less evidence of deer, sheep, or fish. In fact, there is so little evidence for wild game that it seems to imply soldiers must have stayed close to the fort for fear of French and Indian raiding parties. They appear to have done very little hunting.

An analysis of the bones from Fort William Henry is being conducted by Jene Romeo for her doctoral dissertation at Hunter College of the City University of New York, and the final breakdowns of meat consumption

by species should prove most interesting. (A preliminary report appears in this book as appendix 2.) This, of course, is not to imply that plants didn't make up a high proportion of the soldiers' diet, but we have found virtually no charred seeds, nut shells, or other vegetal remains. This may be at least partially due to the highly acidic nature of the sandy soil under the fort, but it could also mean that every last scrap of food was consumed during the siege, and nothing went to waste.

7.31. The distal end of a cow humerus (foreleg) in the dump outside the East Curtain Wall of the fort. The arrow points north, and the vertical rod is marked in 10-cm units.

Overview

The nature of archeology has changed radically since the 1950s, not just at Fort William Henry but also at all manner of historical sites that are open to the public. Gifford was expected to move enormous amounts of earth, scooping out the interiors of entire buildings and digging throughout the parade ground so that developers could create level walking areas for visitors. We do not know how he viewed himself and this approach, but ample photographs have survived that show him in the act of discovery, uncovering skeletons and key artifacts, and I believe he thoroughly loved having the opportunity to find so much. After all, working at a famous American historical site, finding literally thousands of artifacts, and always being viewed by thousands of visitors would be a rush for any archeologist. Certainly a contemporary comparison may be made to Jamestown, Virginia, where the ongoing work of William Kelso and the Jamestown Rediscovery Project has generated enormous popular support and interest, and where every dig is open to viewing by the public (Kelso 2006).

Sixty years have passed since Gifford's excavations, and the scale of modern archeology is decidedly smaller and the amount of record keeping far greater. We have learned that with the discovery of great quantities of artifacts comes an enormous responsibility to have professional conservators stabilize everything that is found; to store all artifacts in secure, temperature-controlled facilities; and to publish virtually everything. In effect, we have truly become preservationists, but years of experience have also shown us that the proper management of artifact collections can be costly. One of the central reasons we dig less today is that everything has a price, and the long-term curation of artifact collections is not cheap.

Gifford uncovered thousands of large, relatively intact artifacts, whereas our modern, more cautious digs produce thousands of small fragments, often in areas that had previously been dug. Perhaps we should feel a bit of envy for what Gifford was able to accomplish, but that really is not the case. Modern archeologists are able to learn just as much from small fragments as we do from complete objects, and we feel the thrill of discovery either way. Since 1997 we have recovered ample period artifacts — the remains of everyday life — scattered everywhere we have dug at Fort William Henry, and it will be exciting to incorporate these new discoveries into future exhibits at the fort. But we also have the satisfaction of knowing that any archeologists who come here in the future will still have much to work with because our small test pits have cautiously sampled each region of the fort, leaving much for future generations to discover. In particular, the dump outside the East Curtain Wall of the fort still holds many wonderful finds, and these will furnish great stories for the next generation of archeologists.

Why Is Fort William Henry Relevant Today?

8

AFTER PURCHASING THEIR TICKETS, modern visitors to Fort William Henry walk across the parade ground to the audiovisual room and watch an introductory film that provides a context for everything that they will see and experience over the next one to two hours. After seeing the film, they embark on a guided tour through the fort, led by an interpreter in uniform (fig. 8.1); they will hear about eighteenth-century life inside Fort William Henry; they will see cannon and musket firing and a grenadier bomb toss; a great many will put their head and hands into the stocks to have their pictures taken (fig. 8.2); and, if they're especially lucky, some will see some archeologists at work (fig. 8.3). A visit to the gift shop (called the Sutler Shoppe) will complete the visit, perhaps with the purchase of some eighteenth-century-style souvenirs (fig. 8.4).

We believe this is an excellent way to gain an almost firsthand experience of many aspects of military life in the 1750s. Unfortunately, other efforts have sometimes not been as effective in telling the story of America's colonial wars. In 2006 many of us viewed an original series on the Public Broadcasting Service titled *The War That Made America*, a selection of stories and programs about sites that focused on the French and Indian War. Although commendable in concept, the setting for most of the events of the war was given as western Pennsylvania (and points even further west), and George Washington was placed at the center of the conflict, even though he had virtually no involvement in the war after 1755. Many people enjoyed this series, but I would argue that it failed to even acknowledge many of the most significant events of the war, which was fought chiefly along the Atlantic coast. Other events were depicted in an amateurish way, such as the battle for Fort Ticonderoga in 1758, which was portrayed by a handful of reenactors fighting on either side of a large brush pile. The largest British encampment of the war, located in Fort Edward, New York, went unmentioned, and also ignored were the various Ranger companies that still evoke some of the most exciting commentary about the war today. Fort William Henry fared little better, and the infamous massacre was never even mentioned. In fact, a Native American actor (Graham Greene) was recruited to tell the story of

8.1. The beginning of a guided tour in 2012 outside the door of the audiovisual room.

8.2. Archeology students put their heads and hands in the stocks at Fort William Henry.

the fort and to claim that only about sixty soldiers had died after nearly a week of intensive fighting.

Why does the French and Indian War receive such poor or inadequate treatment in the United States today? Why are younger generations presented with so little information that is accurate, interesting, and provocative? Although popular television programming is necessarily selective, I would argue that presenting the story of one fort and the dramatic events that occurred there may actually be the most effective way to reveal the motivations, difficulties, and conflicts that were very much at the heart of

8.3. A young visitor in 2011 finds out how dirt is screened for artifacts. The fort's curator, Lauren Sheridan, is at the sifting screen.

the French and Indian War. In the case of Fort William Henry, I also believe that sixty years of archeological research has proved to be a highly effective tool for adding to the traditional, historical account of the siege and massacre. In fact, although archeology was once primarily an aid to site reconstruction, it has increasingly become the only tool that really says anything new about this time period.

But which stories do we tell in publications and in exhibits at Fort William Henry? We find that today many people harbor intense feelings about the massacre. Even after 250 years, many care passionately about how we tell the story. Perhaps the fort's legacy today rests most strongly with the thousands of living descendants of soldiers who served at camps on Lake George, virtually all of whom want the story to be told in a way that shows their ancestors in the most favorable light. And needless to say, we have an enormous backdrop of history and myth against which to tell new stories about Fort William Henry, the massacre, and its aftermath.

In looking at the big picture, we can all agree that Fort William Henry was occupied by a small British garrison whose members were fighting for their lives, and that after the surrender there was a level of ineptitude by the French leadership that outrages audiences even today. To promise safety to your enemies in order to entice them to surrender, and then to allow them to be slaughtered, continues to be deeply disturbing. James Fenimore Cooper was able to take some of these contradictions and animosities and turn them into a rousing love story. There also is much irony in the fact

8.4. The Sutler Shoppe, where visitors may purchase everything from T-shirts to reproduction muskets.

that characterizations of Native Americans in the eighteenth and nineteenth centuries made them the major villains of the story, whereas today they are receiving a much more sympathetic portrayal. By adding modern scientific methods to traditional historical research, we are increasingly recognizing the roles that Native Americans played on both sides of the conflict. Burial 14 was found in the fort's cemetery in 1995 and identified as a Native American in 2012, which is but the latest evidence that Native Americans were valued allies and scouts for the British army.

Everyone's "truth" is different, and not everyone will be satisfied as Fort William Henry, aided by modern archeology, creates new exhibits and stories for modern visitors. Still, we do not want to create a mythology of our own. As we greet the visiting public, we want to be absolutely clear about what is fact, fiction, or simply the best interpretation at the moment. Historians who have told and retold the story of Fort William Henry, and the scholars who have reinterpreted the fort's history, have generally all used the same documents. I would argue that archeologists begin with these same documents, but because we also study stratigraphy, context, and material culture, we seek to tell a richer set of stories that will help make the fort more real for visitors. Every archeologist is, after all, a storyteller. We are visual and tactile in the way we approach our work, and we truly want visitors to enjoy the time they spend with us.

The story of Fort William Henry is tragic and poignant, but as we look back over the years, we are drawn to the inevitable conclusion that this fort symbolizes the harshness and cruelties of life on the early American frontier. We are able to unearth the charred remains of British military buildings, the broken glasses and bowls from officers' dinner tables, and the shattered fragments of mortar bombs that careened through the parade ground during the final siege. The French clearly won a battle on August 9, 1757, but they ultimately lost the war and their claims to the American continent. The fall of Fort William Henry no doubt had a galvanizing effect upon British soldiers and civilians who wanted revenge on the opponents who had betrayed the fort's defenders and let them be massacred.

The sacrifices made by British and provincial soldiers at sites like Fort William Henry were part of a determined campaign against the French and Indians, and ultimately they helped lead to a British victory on the Plains of Abraham outside Quebec City in September 1759. I believe that the soldiers and officers who lived and fought at Fort William Henry were most likely very much like us, and their sacrifices helped us become the Americans we are today. This is not a site from a dead, forgotten war. Rather, this is where our ancestors fought to maintain their identity as an English-speaking people and where they fought to keep English customs and laws. We can be very proud of what they sought to accomplish here on the shores of Lake George.

The Exhibits at Fort William Henry

The Fort William Henry Museum opened to the public in 1955, and its most important goal has always been to tell a story that is accurate and relevant to audiences with ever-changing tastes. As many as 60,000 visitors passed through the reconstructed fort every summer in the 1960s, and many had grown up with *The Last of the Mohicans* story, believing it to be a faithful account of the events that occurred on Lake George in the summer of 1757. However, a great many of today's visitors know extremely little about the French and Indian War, its leaders, battle sites, or its impact on future generations of Americans. That gives staff at the museum about two hours at best to make seemingly distant historical events come alive for visitors of all ages and national backgrounds.

In the first exhibits that were created inside the reconstructed barracks buildings in 1955, Fort William Henry displayed many of the best artifacts that Stanley Gifford had just unearthed from the charred ruins of the fort. Nearly all of the exhibits were the product of intensive archeological research, and history alone could not have provided such a fascinating array of materials that were worn, used, and consumed by the soldiers who actually had lived at the fort. Visitors loved the exhibits, including an extensive firearms collection (fig. A.1). And many of the cases were equipped with tape cartridges that would play two minutes' worth of narration about the items on display inside, which made Fort William Henry the most up-to-date military museum in the region. Perhaps what made the exhibits in the 1950s the strongest were the many colorful dioramas and mannequins that were the creation of John "Jack" Binder, a prominent commercial artist.

Unfortunately, many of the original artifacts were destroyed when an arsonist set fire to the West Barracks on September 18, 1967 (fig. A.2). A replacement building had to be constructed by the beginning of the 1968 season, at a cost of $350,000, and it was necessary to find new artifacts for the new displays. At that time a local newspaper noted: "Using advanced techniques of display which combine the use of all human sensory inputs, the new 5,100 square foot museum area is considered one of the finest in the Northeast" ("State Historian Visits Fort William Henry Restoration" 1968).

A.1. An exhibit of firearms on the first floor of the West Barracks before the fire. Fort William Henry Museum.

A.2. The first floor of the West Barracks after the fire in 1967. Fort William Henry Museum.

Many other exhibits have come and gone since that time, reflecting the obligation of every museum to constantly modernize and tell new stories to visitors. One of the most notable past exhibits was a display of bateaux that had been found by divers in Lake George.

The fort's curators, often assisted by friends and consultants, have always had the responsibility of creating exciting new exhibits. In 1953 Stanley Gifford became the first curator, followed sequentially by Lieutenant Colonel Charles Briggs, Robert Lord, James Magee, Michael Palumbo, Gerald Bradfield, and Lauren Sheridan. Each curator has made it a priority to provide the museum visitor with a balanced perspective on the motivations, tactics, and daily lives of the British, provincial, French, and Native American forces

A.3. The first displays that greet visitors as they enter the reconstructed fort (2013).

A.4. Extensive exhibits in the entryway of the fort (2013).

that served or fought at the fort. This is especially true as the museum seeks to tell the story of the massacre: What were the motivations for it? How have perceptions of the story changed over 250 years? Do we blame Native Americans for their active role in what occurred, or do we blame the French for not adequately protecting their prisoners? Could the massacre have been avoided if Native Americans had been allowed a share of the spoils after the surrender? These are some of the more controversial questions that the museum's exhibits need to address.

The Exhibit Areas

As visitors enter the Fort William Henry Museum, they are greeted by tasteful displays of artifacts, photographs, cannons, and Jack Binder's mannequins (figs. A.3 and A.4). They then proceed to view extensive exhibits on the

A.5. The "Temporary Museum" on the fort grounds during the 1953–54 excavations. Fort William Henry Museum.

A.6. The current arrangement of display cases on the first floor of the West Barracks (2013).

A.7. A wall panel commemorating *The Last of the Mohicans* movies (2013).

A.8. A recreated soldiers' barracks on the second floor of the West Barracks.

first and second floors of the reconstructed West and North Barracks; on the first floor of the East and South Barracks; throughout the parade ground; and in the Cemetery Building southwest of the fort. Visitors are able to view all exhibits at their own pace, separate from the guided tours that feature active demonstrations such as a grenade toss, cannon firing, musket firing, and the casting of musket balls.

While excavations continued in the 1950s, Stanley Gifford required his excavators to place artifacts in open boxes for visitors to see (Carleton Dunn, personal communication, August 15, 2013), and these were on display inside a temporary museum building (fig. A.5). The reconstructed West Barracks subsequently became the principal exhibit area at the fort, with display cases on the first floor that trace the story of the Fort William Henry property from prehistoric times up through the nineteenth century (fig. A.6). Many artifacts excavated in the 1950s are on display here, and for many years a lecture room on this level projected the 1936 film *The Last of the Mohicans*, starring Randolph Scott. Although the film is no longer shown, wall panels about the historical novel and its movie adaptations remain (fig. A.7), and clearly James Fenimore Cooper's story will always be featured in exhibits at the fort. There is also the new Dawn L. Littrell Archaeology and Research Library on the first floor of the West Barracks.

On the second floor of the West Barracks is a large area that is devoted to life in the barracks. It is furnished with bunks, tables, and benches, and it features Jack Binder mannequins shown playing cards and eating (fig. A.8). On the cellar level of the same barracks there is a row of prison cells, a guard room, and an enormous fireplace that stood within the original cellar of the West Barracks (fig. A.9).

A.9. An original barracks fireplace, now in the cellar of the reconstructed West Barracks (2013).

The North Barracks features an exhibit dedicated to Father Isaac Jogues and his discovery of Lake George (Lac du St. Sacrement) in 1646; the recreated office of Colonel Monro; an exhibit on eighteenth-century medicine; an exhibit on "Frontier Life," featuring women who are baking and weaving (fig. A.10); and an exhibit on "Eighteenth-Century Tradesmen" featuring various craft activities (fig. A.11). There are also pictures and artifacts from early nineteenth-century hotels on Lake George. Just to the east of this barracks is a powder magazine, where cannon balls and powder kegs were stored.

The East Barracks contains the fort's audiovisual room, where tours of the fort begin every hour, and there is a Native American room with both historic and prehistoric artifacts on display. A reconstructed Iroquois longhouse helps tell the story of Native Americans in central and western New York State, and the most recent addition is a collection of furs from the several fur-bearing mammals that would have been trapped by Native Americans throughout the region (fig. A.12). Visitors have the opportunity to touch these furs, thereby appreciating why early Americans so prized these animals. Given the importance of Native peoples to the Lake George region, new exhibits were created for the room for 2014.

The South Barracks formerly had changing exhibits, but in 1998 it became the fort's Archeology Room, when curator Gerald Bradfield recreated the fort's well in this room and added many of the more recent artifacts that had been discovered in the well in 1997. For years an adjacent television monitor showed footage of me digging inside the well, and other exhibits in the room featured prehistoric and military artifacts, muskets, and pictures of the 1950s digs. This room received a major updating in 2008, with exhib-

A.10. (*Top*) An exhibit commemorating "Frontier Life."

A.11. (*Middle*) Craftsmen at work in the exhibit on "Eighteenth-Century Tradesmen."

A.12. (*Bottom*) Furs on display in the Native American room. From left to right: fox, wolf, bobcat, beaver, raccoon, skunk, weasel, and otter (2013).

A.13. Representative exhibits in the John Farrell Archaeology Exhibit (2013).

its on the techniques of archeology and forensic anthropology, and large television monitors showing past archeological work at the fort. In 2012 the Archeology Room became the Underwater Archeology Room, with help from Joseph Zarzinski, John Farrell, and Bateaux Below Inc., and in late 2013 this was renamed the John Farrell Archaeology Exhibit. Scale models, television monitors, anchors, and other artifacts help tell the story of navigation and underwater archeology in Lake George, and this is currently the most modern exhibit area at the fort (fig. A.13).

Stepping outdoors into the parade ground (fig. A.14), visitors encounter a whipping post, two pillories (stocks), the original 1756 well, a simulated dig site for children, an archery target, a garden, cannons, a platform where musket balls are cast, areas for craft demonstrations, and "The Crypt," where large photographs and a video have replaced the skeletons of earlier times. These attractions are as entertaining as they are educational, and visitors enjoy photographing each other with head and hands secured in the pillories.

The Cemetery Building is the one exhibit area that visitors may see without having to pay for admission into the fort. The ten skeletons that Stanley Gifford exposed in 1953 were on display until 1993 (see chapter 6), and now large photographs mounted on the walls of the building show physical anthropologists conducting research on the skeletons (fig. A.15). Many visitors

A.14. Looking northeast across the fort's parade ground, with the children's Archeology Dig on the left and the North Barracks in the rear (2013).

A.15. The interior of the Cemetery Building (2013).

still wish to see the bones of soldiers displayed here, but the Fort William Henry Museum believes that it is essential to be respectful of the remains of the dead.

Future Directions

Every museum needs changing attractions so that visitors will want to return, so although some exhibits at the Fort William Henry Museum are relatively permanent, others are updated or replaced every few years. To accelerate changes to the exhibits, in 2012 the collections and the exhibits were placed in the keeping of the French and Indian War Society, a friends' group, which is eager to see the fort recognized as the best attraction on Lake George and, ultimately, as the best historic attraction in northern New York State.

Modern audiences expect interactive exhibits, computer and video screens, and a true "you are there" experience. The ideal might well be a "Time Tunnel" such as that pioneered at the Jorvik Viking Centre in York, England. At Fort William Henry, visitors could go back in time by entering a series of rooms, with the first featuring an Indian camp; another would have soldiers living inside a barracks; another might have archeologists digging the ruins of the fort in the 1950s; and still another might feature an archeology laboratory. As the visitors traveled back in time, they would find themselves encountering each of the successive groups of people who occupied this site. To make this experience as real as possible, the mannequins in each room would be accompanied by the sounds and smells relating to the time period and activity presented.

Perhaps the greatest changes will need to occur in the Native American room, where mannequins would be shown making pottery and cleaning fish and gathered around one of the roasting platforms discovered by archeologists at the fort. Above all, Mohican culture should be stressed. The Mohicans were the first people to occupy the Lake George area, and it would be most appropriate to display modern ethnographic items loaned from the Stockbridge-Munsee Band of the Mohican Nation and to include videos of Mohican dances and other activities as performed today. The "Last" of the Mohicans is a misnomer, and the Fort William Henry Museum has a wonderful opportunity to demonstrate how very alive the Mohican Nation is today.

Other new exhibits might include a fuller story of the excavation and reconstruction of the fort in the 1950s, so that visitors could see for themselves how the modern fort came to be. Many visitors ask: "How accurate is this reconstruction?" New exhibits could more clearly show how engineers' maps in the 1750s, coupled with modern archeology, helped make the recreation a very faithful one. The story of underwater archeology on Lake George is already receiving a great deal of attention, but more could be done with forensics and the story of early medicine. There seems to be a universal fascination with diseases such as smallpox and measles, and one of the most important stories at the fort — which exhibits should address prominently — is how smallpox contracted here by Native Americans subsequently destroyed whole nations when the infected people returned to their homes in Canada.

Just as important is the need to tell more stories about the routines of daily life in Fort William Henry, so modern visitors can identify more closely with those who lived here over 250 years ago. What was it like for a British soldier to serve here? A British officer? A Provincial soldier? A French soldier? A Ranger? Given the modern desire to see live action at all times, it would be useful to incorporate videos of modern reenactors embodying each of these roles, or even to present three-dimensional holograms of each of the protagonists at the fort. It would surely be a thrill for a modern visitor to push a button and both see and hear General Montcalm describing his reactions to the massacre, or listen to a lowly private describe the tedium of daily life.

In the years ahead, the museum's exhibits will continue to change as the staff tries to meet the needs of future visitors. Visitors want good storytelling, and they want to know why a log fort on the shore of Lake George was an essential part of American history. The exhibits in the Fort William Henry Museum have the power to demonstrate that this is a very special place.

Foodways at Fort William Henry: An Interim Progress Report

JENE C. ROMEO

Introduction

Archeological investigations at Fort William Henry in 1997–2000 and 2011–12 uncovered nearly 38,000 faunal remains. The map of the fort included here illustrates the approximate locations of each of the sites that were dug. The site numbers that are used here (and appear in table A.1) are the numbers that appeared in *Massacre at Fort William Henry* (Starbuck 2002). Table A.1 lists the thirteen sites and gives their years of excavation, a brief description of each site, and the number of animal bones found there.

At present the animal bones are being measured, and the bone type and animal species, age, size, sex, and so forth are being identified wherever possible. The bones are also being examined for any alterations caused by nature (weathering, soil acids, and so on), animals (for example, gnawing by a rodent or carnivore), or human activity (butchering, cooking, tool making, decorative work, and so forth). Butchering marks include knife cuts, cleaver chops, and saw marks. Cooking is indicated when a bone has been burned or boiled and shows signs of food extraction, including having been chopped and smashed for marrow. Indeed, butchering and cooking marks predominate as physical evidence that most of the bones so far examined were used for food. But one bone found in site #10, a possible breastwork area in the parking lot, is clearly a piece of worked bone. It appears to have been shaped for decorative purposes, but more research needs to be done before we can be certain about that.

Faunal remains from Fort William Henry may be challenging to interpret for many reasons. We are essentially examining the remains or leftovers of the fort site after the larger, more important items have been removed — often long ago, and with minimal disclosure of where or what was found. The recent excavations show the effects of war, general looting, and unsupervised digs. The site retains the residue of a broad range of occupants (including soldiers, civilians, and Indians) and of tourists over time. The

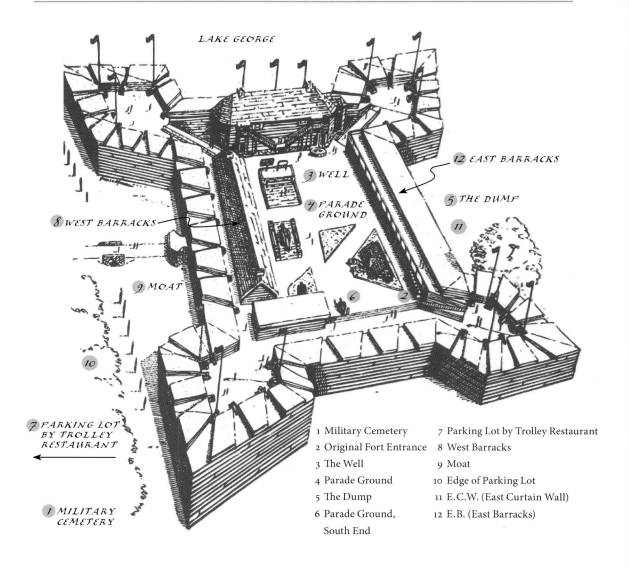

LAKE GEORGE

12 EAST BARRACKS

3 WELL

5 THE DUMP

8 WEST BARRACKS

4 PARADE GROUND

11

9 MOAT

6

2

10

7 PARKING LOT BY TROLLEY RESTAURANT

1 MILITARY CEMETERY

1 Military Cemetery	7 Parking Lot by Trolley Restaurant
2 Original Fort Entrance	8 West Barracks
3 The Well	9 Moat
4 Parade Ground	10 Edge of Parking Lot
5 The Dump	11 E.C.W. (East Curtain Wall)
6 Parade Ground, South End	12 E.B. (East Barracks)

Fort William Henry Site Location Map

fort has been burned twice and been rebuilt and reconfigured. As a result of multiple disturbances, there is little reliable stratigraphy — only limited analysis by layers, levels, or depth — and no secure proveniences through which to reliably connect the bones to specific artifacts with any accuracy, especially after 260 years.

Fort Life

Despite these conditions, the animal bones are able to provide significant information. The sites with the greatest number of faunal remains are the north end of the parade ground (site #4), with 4,480 bones; the dump east of the fort (site #5), with 16,523 bones; the West Barracks (site #8), with 7,601 bones; and the East Curtain Wall, with 4,721 bones. These findings raise questions about human behavior and area use at the fort.

The East Curtain Wall (E.C.W.) is an extension of site #5, and both are generally referred to as "The Dump." Together these two sites generated a combined total of 21,244 bones. But these numbers represent just one dump area, probably the main one, of which only about 5–10 percent has been dug. Where are the other dumps? Several other dumps would have been necessary — based on the number of people living in the fort and the amount of garbage that would have been generated — and must exist. Although all types of garbage are found here, food remains predominate. What is surprising are the very large chunks of bone that have been preserved. Was this area also used as the fort's butchering site? Its location just outside the east entrance to the fort would have been both practical and convenient for that purpose. One must wonder how such large cuts of meat might have been used. Were they destined for the hospital to be cooked in one big pot, feeding those too ill to feed themselves individually? (Thus far, no large pots have been found by archeologists.)

Sites #4 (north end of the parade ground) and #8 (the West Barracks) also produced high numbers of bones from food remains that duplicate the same range of domesticated species (cow, pig, and sheep) that are found in the dump east of the East Curtain Wall. However, these bones represent much smaller cuts of meat compared to those found at the East Curtain Wall and site #5. Do these smaller cuts represent food cooked by individuals or perhaps a few soldiers cooking together to share the task? Both sites #4 and 8 are associated with more domestic artifacts, such as tableware, wine bottle fragments, combs, and pins, which are the ordinary stuff of daily living. We hope the bone analysis will provide some explanation of the differences in bone remains among these four sites.

Foodways

The faunal remains may also serve to complement documentary evidence from personal diaries, officers' orderly books, and military journals. Some food patterns are observable even this early in the bone analysis. Although we cannot distinguish fresh meat from salted, it is clear that cow bones predominate among the refuse and thus cows represent the primary meat source at the fort. Pork was the second most important meat, followed by mutton — both pigs and sheep seem to have been present in significantly lower numbers. Mutton was supposed to be reserved for the sick and, although it was always present, it was not included as standard daily rations (Anderson 1984, 84–87). These initial findings of what I call the protein triumvirate reflect the meat patterns of the regimented British supply system that standardized the military food allowances for British and provincial soldiers alike in 1756.

Wild Faunal Remains

Despite the predominance of domesticated animals in the Fort William Henry archeological faunal record, various wild animals were expected to be present in significant numbers. According to many historical accounts, edible wild fauna was quite plentiful around the fort and in the Lake George area. Many describe great success in hunting and fishing. One soldier wrote: "The Deer continue plenty. . . . Col. Whitcomb this day got seven" (quoted in Kemmer 1997, 21). However, despite the apparent great success in hunting deer, an unexpectedly low number of deer bones have been recovered. Perhaps the men cooked and ate their venison away from the fort as a supplement to their diet. Or those food remains may have been dumped in an area that has not yet been excavated. Small animals such as rabbits, squirrels, and opossums appear to be missing from the excavated sites. Like the deer, they may have been caught, consumed, and disposed of elsewhere, leaving no bones to mark their passing. Wild birds are present, although in limited numbers. As yet there is no evidence of domesticated fowl at the fort. Fish are also scarce among the bones. In 1755, Caleb Rea, the regimental surgeon, wrote about how he enjoyed fishing on Lake George. After one successful fishing trip on the lake, he reported that he had "caught Oswego bass, perch, roach, trouts, etc. but ye bass is ye biggest and counted ye best" (quoted in Kemmer 1997, 21–22). It may be possible to identify the species of the few fish vertebrae that have been recovered.

Not everyone had the pleasure of hunting or fishing. The provincial soldiers had heavy fatigue duty, such as cutting down trees, digging trenches, and building roads, forts, barracks, wharves, boats, and so on. One exhausted

	TABLE A.1. Numbers of Animal Bones Found at Fort William Henry by Site		
Site	Description	Years of excavation	Bone count
#1	Edge of military cemetery	1997, 1998	666
#2	Parade ground, SE corner	1997	469
#3	Well	1997	224
#4	Parade ground, north end	1997	4,480
#5	Dump (East Curtain Wall)	1997, 1998, 1999	16,523
#6	Parade ground, south end	1998	399
#7	Parking lot by Trolley Restaurant	1998	26
#8	West Barracks	1998, 1999, 2000	7,601
#9	Moat on west side of fort	1999	36
#10	Parking lot west of fort	1999	65
E.C.W.	East Curtain Wall	2011, 2012	4,721
E.B.	East Barracks	2011, 2012	2,411
#13	Lawn near Tower Theatre	2000	124
Total			37,745

soldier stated: "Our duty is so hard that our men scarcely have time to cook their victuals or wash their clothes" (quoted in Kemmer 1997, 52). These same soldiers were also expected to drill and train despite their long hours of heavy labor. This was necessary because many provincials were hurt or killed in accidental shootings (Kemmer 1997, 52–53). Many of these soldiers had never handled a gun before signing up, and therefore it would have been dangerous to let them go hunting.

Conclusion

Faunal analysis provides a way to reconstruct life at Fort William Henry through the complexity of the site's military foodways. Information from the animal bones can be compared to that in historical documents, adding depth to current research. It is through the patterns of human behavior that we hope to better understand how the garrison at Fort William Henry functioned, both within the fort and out in the environment it sought to control.

Major General Daniel Webb's Surrender Letter, August 17, 1757

Few British commanders in early America are now as controversial, or disrespected, as Major General Daniel Webb, commander of both Fort Edward and Fort William Henry in 1757. Webb had done little to prepare for the French attack, and it is unclear why — while some of his units were besieged at Fort William Henry — he remained in Fort Edward with a sizable army and sent no additional aid. Was Webb a coward, or was he a practical strategist who realized that he needed to remain entrenched at his most secure position or risk losing his entire command?

It is hard today to determine all of the motivations behind Webb's actions — and inaction — but we do have the letter that he sent to his superior, Lord Loudoun, on August 17, 1757, explaining the loss of Fort William Henry. His letter appears below and reveals what Webb considered to be justifications for his own actions.

> Fort Edward August 17
> 1757.

My Lord

I am sorry the first letter I have the honor of addressing to your Lordship should be to acquaint you of the unfortunate loss of Fort William Henry; to give your Lordship as clear an account of which, as lies in my power, I shall enumerate the most material circumstances that have happened from the first appearance of the Enemy upon Lake George.

> Saturday the 23rd of July

Colonial Parker of the New Jersey Regiment having obtained leave from Lieutenant Colonel Monro who commanded at that Fort, to set out with the three hundred men in twenty seven boats of different kinds to reconnoiter the advanced Guard of the Enemy. At day break the next morning fall in with a Superior number of French and Indians, about twenty six miles down the Lake, who cut off the whole party excepting about fifty who escaped with Colonel Parker, and about fifty more through the woods: on receiving this intelligence the 24th at eight, I set off the next morning with the principle officers and Engineers for Fort William Henry, and having made the best disposition for the Defense of the place that the situation would admit of, and having sent off two whale boats the 28th to reconnoiter the Enemy, who brought word that they were within twelve miles of the Fort, I returned again to Fort Edward the 29th, and immediately wrote the most pressing letter to the several Governors to put their Militia in arms, and join me as fast as possible.

Monday August the 2d Lieutenant Colonel Young with two hundred of the Royal Americans and independents, eight hundred Provincials, six pieces of Cannon and a Detachment of Artillery under the Command of Captain McCloud, marched to Fort William Henry to join the Troops before there under Col. Monro; and after having thrown in the proper Garrison, retrench themselves upon the eminence on the South East, which entirely Commanded the Fort. Tuesday the 3rd, in the evening, I received a letter from Colonel Monro by a Ranger, in which he acquainted me of the Enemy having landed that morning on the west side of the lake, that they had cannon with them; and the Rangers acquainted me that the Fort and Camp were entirely surrounded by a large body of French and Indians, and that it was with the greatest difficulty he could get by, as the woods were full of them. Notwithstanding repeated expresses to the several Governments, no reinforcement of the militia was yet arrived, and the Troops remaining under my command at this place, did not exceed one thousand six hundred men, exclusive of the artificers employed on the works, and the different Commands at Albany and the Posts on Hudsons River, which were immediately ordered up; The Strength of the Camp, and Garrison at Fort William Henry after the last reinforcement, amounted to about two thousand fit for Duty, exclusive of artificers and Sailors, which were taken from the Troops, and were intended for the Galliots that were almost finished, but neither of them launched before the arrival of the Enemy. On the evening of the enemys landing, a scouting party that I sent out in the morning returned with a prisoner, a Lieutenant of Canadians who was of the Investing Party; a Copy of whose information I herewith inclose your Lordship, by which, you will see it was out of my power to give them any assistance at the Fort with the handful of men that remained with me, and the intelligence he gave me, with regard to their strength and artillery proved minutely true.

Saturday the 6th, the Enemy opened a Battery of nine pieces of Cannon on the west end of the lake, from which they kept a constant fire on the Fort but did not do them much hurt; the Commands at the different posts being now come in, augmented our numbers at this place to two thousand five hundred men, comprehending artificers, and every man that was able to bear arms; this day about five hundred of the militia under Sir William Johnson arrived, and about an hundred and fifty Indians of different Tribes, and Nations; but not to tire your Lordship with unnecessary occurrences, the Enemy having opened another Battery of nine pieces of cannon on the eighth, and the Garrison of the Fort having all their heavy Cannon and two Mortars burst, which were their principal pieces of artillery, and the Enemy having on the 9th in the morning another Battery ready to open within an hundred and fifty yards of the ditch, and the inside of the Fort being on fire all the night before with their shells, they were obliged to Capitulate, nor was it ever in my power to march to their relief, as the day of the surrender, there were counted but two thousand three hundred of the Militia, with which, and the other Troops under my command, the greatest part of which were Provincials, I did not think it prudent to risk a battle against such superior force, as the consequence of a defeat, must have exposed this Fort and the whole Province to the Incursions of the Enemy. Enclosed I send your Lordship the Copy of the articles of Capitulation, notwithstanding which, as soon as the Fort was evacuated by our Troops, the sick and wounded were murdered by the Indians, and altho' both Officers and men, agreeable to the desire of the French, had given up all their baggage and effects to satisfie the Indians, they were attacked on their return to this place. Wednesday the 10th, every man strip'd of the cloaths he had on his back, several men, women, and children, murdered, scalped, and carried of Prisoners, besides others who must have perished in the woods, to which they run for shelter from these Barbarities; during this inhuman behavior, which was within sight of the Camp, the Escort of the French were looking on. Colonel Monro, with several other Officers, and about four hundred men, returned to the Fort and put themselves under the immediate protection of M. Montcalm, and arrived here the 14th. The rest who saved themselves by flight, have continued coming in daily from the woods, in which many of them must have perished with hunger.

After having destroyed the Fort, and sent off the provisions, ammunition, and artillery that remained therein, to Carillion; M. Montcalm set off yesterday about twelve with his whole Army; nor was it ever in my power to attack him, so the greatest number of Militia I could by repeated expresses collect at this place, did not amount to above four thousand men; with such as would stay / and I must here do Sir William Johnson the Justice to say he was indefaticable in his endeavors and Solicitations but to no purpose to detain them / I made a stand at this Fort; tho' had the Enemy proceeded to the attack of it, I see nothing could have prevented its falling into their hands.

Colonel Monro, and all the officers having lost their papers with the rest of their baggage, it is impossible as yet to make out a return of what men we have lost; three officers of the Massachusetts were killed, and Lieutenant Colonel Young of the Royal Americans, Captain Ormsby, and Captain Cunningham of the 35th Regiment wounded, Captain Ormsby as he was not able to travel here is carried to Canada according to the Articles of the Capitulation, and Captain Feesh / but with what Justice I cannot say / taken as Hostage. The other officers and Soldiers I have sent down to Albany that the Articles may be kept on our side, till I shall receive further orders from the Earl of Loudon in what manner they are to act, in consequence of this behavior of the Enemy.

I have wrote to the different Governments immediately to complete the deficiencies in their several Regiments, occasioned by those who were at the Siege of Fort William Henry being by the articles of the Capitulation rendered incapable of serving for the present.

As an opportunity at this time offered of sending your Lordship a return of the Troops under my Command, I thought it my duty to give your Lordship as authentic an account of this affair as it is at present in my power to obtain; as well for the Satisfaction of your Lordship as the Justification of my own conduct therein. I must at the same time do Lt. Colonel Monro and the rest of the Regular Troops who were concerned in this Siege the Justice to say, they behaved extreamly well; and wish it was in my power to alledge as much in favor of the Provincials, who made up the greatest part of their strength.

I am

My Lord,

With great respect

Your Lordships

Most obedient and

Most Humble Servant

Dan. Webb.

Lord Barrington

Endorsed Coll. Webb.

Fort Edward

17th August. 1757.

FURTHER READING

Anderson, Fred. 1984. *A People's Army: Massachusetts Soldiers and Society in the Seven Years War.* Chapel Hill: University of North Carolina Press.

"Archeologists Find Blacksmith Shop of Fort William Henry." *Times-Union* (Albany, NY), August 29, 1954.

Baker, Brenda J., and Christina B. Rieth. 2000. "Beyond the Massacre: Historic and Prehistoric Activity at Fort William Henry." *Northeast Anthropology* 60:45–61.

Bellico, Russell P. 1995. *Chronicles of Lake George: Journeys in War and Peace.* Fleischmanns, NY: Purple Mountain.

———. 2010. *Empires in the Mountains.* Fleischmanns, NY: Purple Mountain.

Blackwell, Jon. 1996. "Late Recognition: Exhuming of Bodies at Fort William Henry Sheds Light on Black Soldiers' Contribution in French and Indian War." *Sunday Gazette* (Schenectady, NY), December 1.

Brown, Margaret Kimball. 1971. "Glass from Fort Michilimackinac: A Classification System for Eighteenth Century Glass." *Michigan Archaeologist* 17 (3–4): 97–215.

Calver, William Louis, and Reginald Pelham Bolton. 1950. *History Written with Pick and Shovel.* New York: New-York Historical Society.

Carola, Chris. 2012. "Last Mohican Skeleton Investigated in Forensic Series." Press release from the Associated Press, March 29. http://www.forensicmag .com/news/2012/03/last-mohican-skeleton-investigated-forensic-series# .UiysymTwL4A.

Coe, Michael D. 2006. *The Line of Forts: Historical Archaeology on the Colonial Frontier of Massachusetts.* Hanover, NH: University Press of New England.

Cooper, James Fenimore. *The Last of the Mohicans.* 1826. Reprint, New York: Penguin, 1980.

Dodge, Edward J. 1998. *Relief Is Greatly Wanted.* Bowie, MD: Heritage.

Dunn, Shirley W. 1994. *The Mohicans and Their Land, 1609–1730.* Fleischmanns, NY: Purple Mountain.

Evans, Lynn. 2003. *Keys to the Past: Archaeological Treasures of Mackinac.* Mackinac Island, MI: Mackinac State Historic Parks.

"Ft. Wm. Henry to Be Rebuilt." 1952. *Times-Union* (Albany, NY). October 24.

Funk, Robert E. 1976. "Recent Contributions to Hudson Valley Prehistory." *New York State Museum Memoir* no. 22. Albany, NY: New York State Museum.

Gifford, Stanley M. 1955. *Fort Wm. Henry — A History.* Lake George, NY: Fort William Henry.

Grimm, Jacob L. 1970. "Archaeological Investigations of Fort Ligonier 1960–1965." *Annals of the Carnegie Museum* 42. Pittsburgh, PA.

Guilday, John. 1970. "Animal Remains from Archaeological Excavations at Fort Ligonier." *Annals of the Carnegie Museu*m 42:177–86.

Hanson, Lee H., Jr., and Dick Ping Hsu. 1975. *Casements and Cannonballs: Archeological Investigations at Fort Stanwix, Rome, New York.* Publications in Archeology 14. National Park Service, Washington, D.C.

Hart, John P., and Christina B. Rieth, eds. 2002. *Northeast Subsistence-Settlement Change, A.D. 700–1300.* New York State Museum Bulletin 496. Albany, NY.

Hughes, Ben. 2011. *The Siege of Fort William Henry.* Yardley, PA: Westholme Publishing, LLC.

Jones, Olive R., and E. Ann Smith. 1985. *Glass of the British Military, ca. 1755–1820.* Studies in Archaeology, Architecture and History. Ottawa, ON: Parks Canada.

Karklins, Karlis, ed. 2000. *Studies in Material Culture Research.* Uniontown, PA: Society for Historical Archaeology and Parks Canada.

Kelso, William M. 2006. *Jamestown: The Buried Truth.* Charlottesville: University of Virginia Press.

Kemmer, Brenton C. 1997. *Freeman, Freeholders, and Citizen Soldiers: An Organizational History of Colonel Jonathan Bagley's Regiment, 1755–1760.* Bowie, MD: Heritage Books, Inc.

Liston, Maria A., and Brenda J. Baker. 1995. "Reconstructing the Massacre at Fort William Henry, New York." *International Journal of Osteoarchaeology* 6:28–41.

McGary, Kathy. 1953. "'Grave Diggers' Busy Restoring Fort William Henry Site." *Schenectady Gazette*, June 5.

Neumann, George C., and Frank J. Kravic. 1975. *Collector's Illustrated Encyclopedia of the American Revolution.* Texarkana, TX: Rebel.

Noel Hume, Ivor. 1969. *A Guide to Artifacts of Colonial America.* New York: Alfred A. Knopf.

Parkman, Francis. 1962. *Montcalm and Wolfe.* With a new introduction by Samuel Eliot Morison. New York: Collier.

Ritchie, William A. 1980. *The Archaeology of New York State.* Harrison, NY: Harbor Hill.

Rogers, Robert. 2002. *The Annotated and Illustrated Journals of Major Robert Rogers.* Annotated and with an introduction by Timothy J. Todish; illustrated and with captions by Gary S. Zaboly. Fleischmanns, NY: Purple Mountain.

Snow, Dean R. 1977. "The Archaic of the Lake George Region." In *Amerinds and Their Paleoenvironments in Northeastern North America*, edited by Walter Newman and Bert Salwen, 431–38. New York: New York Academy of Sciences.

———. 1980. *The Archaeology of New England.* New York: Academic Press.

Starbuck, David R. 1990. "A Retrospective on Archaeology at Fort William Henry, 1952–1993: Retelling the Tale of *The Last of the Mohicans*." *Northeast Historical Archaeology* 20:8–26.

———. 1993. "Anatomy of a Massacre." *Archaeology* 46 (November–December): 42–46.

———. 1998. "The Big Dig: Looking for Traces of Fort William Henry's Brutal

Past." *Adirondack Life* 29 (September–October): 44–49, 77–78.

———. 1999a. "Early Military Sites Archaeology in New York State: An Interview with Richard J. Koke." *Northeast Historical Archaeology* 28:71–88.

———. 1999b. *The Great Warpath*. Hanover, NH: University Press of New England.

———. 2001. "Beneath the Bubblegum." *Archaeology* 54 (January–February): 22–23.

———. 2002. *Massacre at Fort William Henry*. Hanover, NH: University Press of New England.

———. 2004. *Rangers and Redcoats on the Hudson*. Hanover, NH: University Press of New England.

———. 2008. "The 'Massacre' at Fort William Henry: History, Archaeology, and Reenactment." *Expedition* 50:17–25.

———. 2010. *Excavating the Sutlers' House: Artifacts of the British Armies in Fort Edward and Lake George*. Hanover, NH: University Press of New England.

———. 2011. *The Archaeology of Forts and Battlefields*. Gainesville: University Press of Florida.

"State Historian Visits Fort William Henry Restoration." *Glens Falls Times* (Glens Falls, NY), July 27, 1968.

Steele, Ian K. 1990. *Betrayals: Fort William Henry & the "Massacre."* New York: Oxford University Press.

Stone, Lyle M. 1974. *Fort Michilimackinac 1715–1781: An Archaeological Perspective on the Revolutionary Frontier*. Anthropological Series, vol. 2. Michigan State University, East Lansing, in cooperation with Mackinac Island State Park Commission, Mackinac Island, Michigan.

Sullivan, Catherine. 1986. *Legacy of the Machault: A Collection of 18th-Century Artifacts*. Ottawa, ON: Parks Canada.

Todish, Timothy J. 1993. "Triumph and Tragedy: The Siege of Fort William Henry, pt. 2." *Muzzleloader* (January–February):31–36.

Zaboly, Gary Stephen. 2004. *A True Ranger: The Life and Many Wars of Major Robert Rogers*. Garden City Park, NY: Royal Blockhouse.

INDEX

Majot, Sarah, viii, 39
Mamby, William, 79, *79*
massacre, vii, 5–8, 64, 65, 68, 69, 95, 103
McEvoy, Joe, 34
Middlesex Culture, 13
Military Road to Fort Edward, 5, 64
moat, 4, 5, 39–40, *81*, 117
Mohawks, 4, 69
Mohicans, 9, 69, 110
Monro, Lieutenant-Colonel George, 3, 5, 6, *26*, 106, 119–22
Montcalm-Gozon, General Louis-Joseph de, 5, 6, 7, *20*, 64, 111, 121
mortar shells, 23, *23*, 37, 38, 48, *49*, 50, 73, 89, 90, *90*, 99
mouth harps. *See* Jew's harps
musket balls, 23, 31–34, *32*, 37, 41, 48–52, 56, 61, 63, 65, 72, 73, 88, *89*, 105, 108
musket parts, 88, *88*

nails, 85
Native American Graves Protection and Repatriation Act (NAGPRA), 70
Native Americans, ix, 1, 2, 5–7, 9–18, 43, 54, 59, 63, 64, 68–70, 78, 91, 95, 98, 102–3, 106, *107*, 110, 119–21
needles, 37, 79–80, *80*
New Jersey Regiment ("Jersey Blues"), 5, 119
New York State Museum, 65
New York State Office of Parks, Recreation and Historic Preservation, 34

Odanak, 7
ox shoe, 91

Paleo-Indian period, 11
Palumbo, Mike, 29, 102
parade ground, 4, 10, 13–16, 18, 23, 27, 29, 31, 34–35, 39, 44, 73, 75–78, 80, 83–86, 89, 91, 93, 95, 105, 108–9, 115, 117
Parsons, Merle, viii, 71
pins, 37, 50, 79–80, *80*, 115

pipes, tobacco, 23, 31, *32*, 48, 51, 54, 73, 78–79, *79*
postholes, 35, *37*
postmolds. *See* postholes
pottery. *See* ceramics
prehistoric artifacts, 9–18, *10–11, 14–16, 18*, 22, 34, 106
prisoners, 5–7, 103, 121

Quebec City, 7, 99
Queen Anne's War, 4

regiments, American: First Battalion Pennsylvania, 75, *76*; Second Battalion Pennsylvania, 73, 75; 22nd Regiment, 75, *76*
regiments, British: 35th Regiment, 5, 122; 42nd Highlanders, 5; 44th Regiment of Foot, 4, 5; 48th Regiment of Foot, 5
Reynolds, Tony, viii, 68
Rigaud de Vaudreuil, Francois-Pierre de, 5
rings, finger, 35, 78
Ritchie, William A., 13
roasting platform, 13, 15, *15*, 16, 17, 54, 110
Rogers, Captain Richard, 6
Rogers Island, 92
Rogers, Major Robert, 6
Rogers' Rangers, 5, 6, 7, 29, 44
Romeo, Jene, viii, 92, 113–17
Roubaud, Pere Pierre, 64
Rozell, Matthew, viii, *36, 37*, 92, 113–17

Saint Francis, 6, 7
scabbard holder, 88, *88*
scalping, 5–7, 23, *23*, 63
scissors, 37, 50, 79
Scratch Blue, 80, *82*
sewing supplies. *See* needles, pins, thimbles
shell beads. *See* wampum
Sheridan, Lauren, viii, 43, *97*, 102
shovels. *See* spades

smallpox, 6, 60, 68, 110

Snow, Dean R., 12

spades, 45, 73

Speakman's Company, 5

spoons, 23, 37, 73, 83, *85*

sprue. *See* lead sprue

State University of New York
    Adirondack, vii, 9, 25, 29, 43, 65, 71

Steele, Ian K., 1, 5–6

Stockbridge Indians. *See* Mohicans

storehouses, 4

Sutler Shoppe, 95, 98

Taylor, Karen T., viii, 69, *69*

The War That Made America, 95–96

thimbles, 37, 79, *80*

Ticonderoga. *See* Fort Ticonderoga

Tippet, Robert, 79, *79*

Todish, Timothy J., viii, 1

Treaty of Paris, 7

Ulu, 9

Veeder, Harold, 21

wampum, 15, *16*, 78

Washington, General George, 4, 7, 95

Webb, Major General Daniel, 1, 119–22

Weinman, Paul, 12

Weinman site, 12

Weinman, Tom, 12

well, 7, *8*, 29, *30*, 31–34, *32–33*, 90, 91, 106, 108, 117

Williams, Colonel Ephraim, 4

Wolfe, Major General James, 7

women, 9, 17, 106

Woodland period, 11, 12, 15, 17, 18

worms, 88, *88*

Zarzynski, Joseph W., viii, 108